Fundamentals of
Jail & Prison

Administrative/Internal
Investigations

Fundamentals of Jail & Prison

Administrative/Internal Investigations

D. P. Lyons

authorHOUSE®

AuthorHouse™
1663 Liberty Drive
Bloomington, IN 47403
www.authorhouse.com
Phone: 1 (800) 839-8640

Published by AuthorHouse   03/28/2015

ISBN: 978-1-5049-0222-9 (sc)
ISBN: 978-1-5049-0221-2 (e)

Print information available on the last page.

Any people depicted in stock imagery provided by Thinkstock are models, and such images are being used for illustrative purposes only. Certain stock imagery © Thinkstock.

This book is printed on acid-free paper.

About the Author

D. P. Lyons is a retired warden having worked in large detention centers and state prisons. He retired from the New York City, Department of Correction at Rikers Island in 1993. After retirement he served as warden of the U.S. Department of Justice, Immigration and Naturalization Center (Wackenhut Corrections Corp.) in Aurora, Colorado, consultant to the Minister of Justice, Antilles, the Netherlands and warden of the Eddy County Adult and Juvenile Detention Centers in Carlsbad, New Mexico. After his second retirement from correctional management, he served as adjunct professor of criminal justice, Rust College, Holly Springs, MS. specializing in criminal investigations and management of correctional institutions. Lyons has undergraduate degrees in Business Administration and Correction Administration from the City University of New York and a Master of Human Services Degree from Lincoln University, Oxford, PA. Lyons also served as principal instructor administrative investigations, correctional supervision and management at the New York City Correction Academy. He co-authored the New York City Department of Correction's first facility internal investigations training manual. The author is published by the American Correctional Association (ACA) on facility internal investigations and formerly served as a reviewer of new manuscripts for publication by the ACA and the International Association of Correctional Officers on correctional operations.

The author's first book published in 2011, entitled, *Where Are the Keepers*, was an investigation into a major New York newspaper report that the N.Y.C. Dept. of Correction had the highest financial expenditure on employee overtime than any other city agency. The investigation resulted in implementation strategies designed by Lyons to assist in the reduction of employee absenteeism and resultant overtime expenditures by ten million dollars in one fiscal year.

Lyons has served as special guest lecturer at the John Jay College of Criminal Justice, in New York City in the criminal investigation course for New York City Transit Police detectives. He also served as special guest lecturer on correctional operations at the New Mexico State University at Carlsbad. The author has approximately thirty years of experience conducting and reviewing supervisory internal investigations.

Contents

Preface

The goal of this book is to provide correctional supervisors and others tasked with the responsibility of conducting internal investigations with the information and tools to become proficient and meet the state and federal court mandates and expectations of quality. The procedures and tasks in this book serve as a proactive means of preventing correctional supervisors from being charged with failure to conduct a proper investigation and/or being part of a cover-up. For correctional managers and others reviewing supervisory investigations this book provides the critical information that you should look for before approving and passing on such investigations. This book is pursuant to correctional case law, expert opinions of authorities in the field of corrections, professional investigative agencies and this author's over thirty years of experience in conducting investigations in law enforcement and corrections.

A needs assessment supported by court decisions, a review of current literature and internal investigation procedures, techniques and written reports reveal that correctional administrative investigations are within the context of superficial, inadequate and fundamentally bias and in many cases are intended for the exoneration of staff. This manual introduces and reinforces procedures, techniques, and standards of state courts, federal courts and professional investigation agencies.

Acknowledgements

I wish to express my sincere appreciation to Jess Maghan, Ph.D, author and retired professor and director, forum for comparative corrections formerly of the University of Chicago. While serving as deputy commissioner of the New York City, Dept. of Correction, (Academy), Dr. Maghan provided motivation, support, encouragement and a professional example of literary excellence that serves as an example for other authors to emulate.

Lincoln University, Master of Human Services Program, Oxford, Pennsylvania. Lincoln University is nationally considered among the best small universities in the United States and continually lives up to its national reputation for outstanding graduate instruction and student self-actualization, especially Doctors Linda Stine, James Maxey III and James Thomas.

Matt Foreman, Attorney at Law and former special assistant to the First Deputy Commissioner, City of New York, Dept. of Correction. Attorney Foreman and I coauthored the first *Facility Investigations Training Manual* accepted for the department by the Commissioner of Correction. Matt Foreman shared his extensive knowledge and also helped to self-actualize this author.

Chapter 1

INTRODUCTION

Chapter Learning Objectives

- Define investigation and its purpose
- Explain the goal of an investigation
- State what the findings of an investigation are used for
- Discuss the problems related to delays in conducting an investigation
- Summarize the steps involved in taking control in emergency incidents
- Restate the preliminary investigation outline
- Discuss the value of note taking

As a correctional investigator you must not make prejudgments or decide in advance who is guilty and who is innocent. Anton Aboud (1986) an authority on conducting facility investigations states that the investigator is neither prosecutor nor judge, he or she is one who scrutinizes, studies, probes, searches, one who examines and inquires with systematic attention and observation to detail and relationship. According to Article 10,of the Canons of Police Ethics: "An investigator seeks to find the truth, not simply to prove suspects guilty". Further, the investigator shall ascertain what constitutes evidence and shall present such evidence impartially and without malice. In so doing, the investigator shall ignore social, political and all other distinctions among person(s) involved. When

I teach investigations to newly promoted correctional supervisors and managers, I constantly reiterate that authorities state that an investigation is "an objective quest for truth".

Continuously reiterating that an investigation is an objective quest for truth is very important because most of the time the facility level investigator will be conducting inquiries into the people that he works with who may be his/her friends and maybe even went through the correction academy together; therefore, objectivity is very important when, and if, your report of investigation is reviewed by judges, attorneys, and civil court juries. To paraphrase the words of a famous judge in the eastern District Court of New York, while listening to testimony or reading reports by inmates or officers the testimony of both are evaluated the same. What tips the scale of credibility to either the inmate or the officer is evidence. Other problems associated with objectivity is that conclusions are made in the investigator's mind but steps that the fact-finder used in reaching that conclusion are not put down in writing. Also, if there are inconsistencies in the inmate participant/witness reports or staff participant/witness reports they are often overlooked. The inconsistencies are not explained and most of the time ignored. Indeed, in <u>Fisher v. Koehler,</u> (1987), approximately one hundred and seventy-five internal investigations were randomly selected from one correctional facility and reviewed by three national authorities on investigations who all agreed that every one should have been thrown out or returned for further investigation or they would have had someone else conduct the investigation due to lack of objectivity and failure to pursue fundamental questions. Indeed inconsistencies were magnified in the inmates' reports but inconsistencies in staff reports were ignored. According to the court, "investigators 'reached' for ways to exonerate staff and discredit inmates". In some instances the investigating officer was a participant in an incident and also investigated it and cleared himself of all wrongdoing and stated compliance with facility policy. In some cases the investigator's findings and conclusions were inconsistent with medical evidence.

Definition

Experts on investigations, namely, Hess and Orthmann (2010) define investigation as "a patient step-by-step inquiry or observation, a careful examination, a recording of evidence or a legal inquiry. It is the process of discovering, collecting, preparing, identifying and presenting evidence to determine what happened and who is responsible". Another definition more simply stated by Antoine Aboud (1986), "An investigation is the collection of information to describe and explain an event or series of events". Adding to the above two authors above, I submit that an investigation is the collection of information to describe and explain an unusual occurrence, allegations, information received from grievances, information obtained from the normal course of routine correctional operations within the detention center or prison that tends to indicate the possibility of criminal violations or departmental violations on the part of inmates, visitors, employees or volunteers. It involves discovering, collecting, preparing, identifying and presenting evidence that is conducted by correctional supervisors or managers to find out what happened, who is responsible, and identifying policy and procedure violations.

Goal of Investigations

As previously stated, the fundamental purpose of any investigation is to find out what happened in a given incident, why an incident occurred, and what can be done to prevent recurrence. The investigator's findings and conclusions as to whether the incident would have occurred if policy was followed and the investigator's findings and conclusions based upon evidence as to what steps should be taken, if any, to prevent the incident from occurring again is critical and necessary information. The investigator's first obligation is to the facts. Those of us old enough to remember the television program, Dragnet will remember police sergeant Joe Friday continuously telling alleged witnesses, *"just the facts madam, just the facts"*, and likewise our obligation is to the facts. Investigators cannot allow issues not related to the

3

facts such as whether a participant is an employee or an inmate, or a participant's race, sex, religion or other non-factual issue affect one's findings, conclusions and recommendations. As the investigator, you are the critical link in maintaining command accountability, compliance with policies and procedures, and you should clean your own house before an inmate's attorney or the state or federal court cleans house for you. I caution investigators to never get caught up in a cover-up.

What are the Findings of an Investigation Used for?

I have personally observed that in some rural detention centers investigations are not conducted when they should be. In prisons and large detention centers conducting investigations are the norm. The administration is setting itself up for a lawsuit by failing to address various types of incidents that may occur within a detention center. For example, an inmate may allege that he was assaulted by a staff member, there are medical injuries consistent with the inmate's complaint on that date and time as reported by the attending medical personnel, or even worse the facility did not provide medical care.

However, there is no rule violation report or report of investigation on the inmate's allegation. This could subject the administration to a lawsuit. In some cases the detention center is under the authority of the county sheriff and jail staff request a law enforcement investigation of an incident. If, and, only if, the investigation is conducted by law enforcement it has been this author's experience that the findings are not shared with the jail staff nor are there any conclusions whether jail policy and procedure was followed in a particular incident including the use of force policy (if there is one) and force avoidance techniques. If the detention center is not conducting an investigation on all unusual occurrences, a word to the wise, start conducting one. The following lists ways that the findings of an investigation are used for.

The findings of an investigation are used to identify perpetrators (wrongdoers), if an inmate attacks another inmate an investigation should be launched to uncover the identity of the attacker so that disciplinary action can be taken and to prevent the inmate from attacking others. Investigation may reveal that the attacker is a predatory inmate who should be reclassified. In regard to the U.S. District Court in <u>U.S. v. Terrell County, Ga.</u> (2006), the federal government brought a Civil Rights of Institutionalized Persons Act claim against a county, county sheriff, and various other county officials, seeking a determination that county jail conditions were grossly deficient in violation of the 14th Amendment. The court determined that the sheriff and other officials responsible for the jail were deliberately indifferent to the jail's gross deficiencies including the area of protection of inmates from harm from other inmates. Prior to that incident it was well established by the U.S. District Court in <u>Hamilton v. Love</u>, (1971), that the only legitimate purpose served by pretrial detention is to assure that defendants are present at trial. Minimally, the detainee ought to have the reasonable expectation that he or she would survive their period of detainment with their life, that they would not be assaulted, abused, or molested during their detainment, and that their physical health would be reasonably protected. I submit the above to say be proactive to avoid inmate litigation against the facility and the government officials responsible for supervising the detention center, one must take some action to identify inmate perpetrators, discipline the individual and take reasonable steps to prevent the incident from occurring again this is where the investigator's findings and recommendations come in.

Investigations are used to retrieve weapons or other contraband, nothing is more dangerous in a detention center or prison than contraband, particularly weapons and drugs. A good investigation and search can not only recover contraband, but also determine how it was introduced into the facility and where it was made inside the facility (in case of weapons). The American Correctional Association (ACA) is a proactive organization for the prevention of inmate law suits by following nationally recognized standards. According to the ACA, the facility should have a policy in place with methods of intercepting moving weapons and other contraband that should include the use of fixed posts with metal detectors, random interception of inmate traffic such as pat frisking inmates going to and coming out of service areas especially an inmate cafeteria and shakedowns of inmate food carts, maintenance carts and so on. In general, strip searches may be conducted where there is a reasonable belief that can be justified in writing by policy and training that an inmate may be in possession of contraband such as weapons or drugs. The purpose of a search is not to harass inmates but to prevent the introduction of weapons or other contraband such as drugs or escape related contraband.

Investigations are used to assist in prosecuting the perpetrator charged with an offense. A facility investigation usually forms the basis for disciplinary action and/or criminal prosecutions. A good investigation helps insure that the guilty are punished. A poorly accomplished investigation helps insure that the guilty are not identified or punished. Inmates should be prosecuted for possession of serious contraband such as narcotics and for serious assaults on staff and other inmates with significant injuries. In this author's experience when inmates are not prosecuted, it sends them a message that nothing will happen to them for serious assaults especially on staff. You will then see a significant increase in the number of assaults on staff and other inmates as well as an increase in narcotic trafficking in the facility. It is therefore recommended that where prosecution is warranted, your recommendation at the end of your report of investigation should respectfully recommend criminal prosecution.

To show the staff who acted properly and those who acted improperly according to facility policy. A thorough investigation will not only identify the perpetrator but will also show whose actions were consistent and/or inconsistent with policy and/or the inmate rules of discipline. In <u>Charles Fisher et al. v. Richard Koehler et. al</u> (1987), as previously mentioned one of the issues of concern was that internal investigations did not state if staff actions were consistent with agency policy especially in cases involving the use of physical force. If staff actions were not pursuant to policy of course the investigator must address the specific issue of non-compliance with rules, regulations and/or approved training.

I guarantee that if the investigator does not identify the rule or training violation it will be addressed by an opposing attorney or the public defender's office. A poor or incomplete investigation may lead a fair and reasonable person to believe that the investigator is trying to "cover up" the incident in order to exonerate staff.

The findings of an investigation are used to make recommendations for inmate discipline or separations, personnel actions or policy changes. An investigation will often uncover the "causes" of an incident and should point to a solution. For example, an investigation may show that two inmates have long-standing animosities or are rival gang members and must be housed separately. It may show that one inmate is controlling others and should be transferred to administrative segregation. It may also show that policies, procedures, classification or the facility activities schedule are contributing factors and should be revised.

Investigations are used to assist supervisors in training and instructing subordinate staff in the proper execution of assigned tasks. An investigation can reveal that line staff helped to contribute to an incident by not following proper procedures or through bad interpersonal communications. It is a supervisor's responsibility to bring such behavior to the attention of their subordinates and correct the negative behavior. When staff have been properly trained (documented) and fail to follow that training it should be considered a need for retraining or progressive discipline.

Delays

Unnecessary delays in conducting an investigation in a correctional institution should be avoided. Evidence is subject to being altered, destroyed, hidden and so on. For example, you may be ordered to conduct an investigation on a Worker's Compensation case where an officer reports that during inclement weather he entered the institution and slipped on water, ice or snow. If you respond immediately to the scene before an inmate is ordered to "get the water up", you may find the physical evidence to wit, black skid marks, water or traces of moisture where the employee slipped and fell. You may also find some eyewitnesses to the incident.

Delays will increase the likelihood that physical evidence will disappear. For example, if you have the responsibility of investigating a particular area of the institution and you hear over the radio an inmate assault in progress you should immediately respond to the area. Upon staff arrival the inmates will usually walk away as if they were not witnesses or participants to the incident. It is usually easy to find the victim of the assault but he may be afraid to name his assailant. An immediate response may reveal within the crowd of inmates an inmate whose clothes are disheveled, torn, or otherwise out of place. He may also be breathing heavily and he may have scratches and bruises. Indeed, if you are in luck, you may even find fresh blood on his clothing or shoes because he did not have a chance to wash up or change clothes. If you ask him to show you the bottom of his shoes he may even have blood on his shoes where he stomped the inmate.

Remember when you write the investigation of the rule violation report you do not need *"guilty beyond a reasonable doubt, you only need* a preponderance of available evidence" that the inmate is probably the assailant. Gifis (1984) reminds investigators that a preponderance of evidence refers to proof which leads the hearing officer (trier of fact) to find that the existence of the fact at issue is more probable than not. This standard of proof is much different from the standard of proof required in a criminal case, that is, clear and convincing evidence and/or guilty beyond a reasonable doubt. We will go into more detail on investigating inmate rule violations reports in Chapter 11.

As previously stated, delay will permit a perpetrator an opportunity to deliberately alter physical evidence in an effort to redirect blame for an incident away from him and/or away from another person the perpetrator may seek to protect by concocting untruths and lining up witnesses willing to support the false testimony.

Most people's memories begin to fail over time, the more time that elapses between an incident and the interview, the greater the chance that the investigator will be given erroneous, exaggerated or false information.

Inmate perpetrators or eyewitnesses may be transferred to another correctional facility and not scheduled to return or they may be bailed out (bonded out) or otherwise discharged from the facility which will result in the loss of their testimonial evidence.

Delays may prevent an investigator from receiving a dying declaration from an inmate. In extreme cases, when it can be reasonably concluded by the investigator after consultation with emergency medical personnel that the inmate has suffered a serious physical injury and may die especially with vicious stabbings that could result in death. The investigator should go with the inmate inside the emergency ambulance while the inmate is being transported and try to obtain a statement (dying declaration) from the inmate if conscious and if permitted by emergency medical personnel. Bernstein (1997), the Suffolk University Law Review, defines a dying declaration as a statement by a person who is conscious and knows that their death is imminent concerning what he or she believes to be the cause or circumstances of death that can be introduced into evidence during a trial in certain cases. Bernstein reports that a dying declaration is considered credible evidence and trustworthy based on the general belief that most people who know that they are about to become deceased do not lie. As a general rule, dying declarations are an exception to the hearsay rule which prohibits the use of a statement made by someone other than the person who reports it while testifying during a trial because of its inherent untruthfulness. The investigator reports the facts as they occur and should not become overly concerned if it is discovered later on at trial that the person who made the dying declaration had the slightest hope of recovery. Another question for the courts, not the investigator, is before admitting a dying declaration obtained by the investigator whether the person who makes a dying declaration is mentally competent at the time he or she makes the statement, otherwise it is inadmissible.

Taking Control in Emergency Situations

Before we get into investigative procedures a word to supervisors responding to emergency incidents that may require them to conduct a preliminary investigation. Before you concern yourself with conducting an investigation it is recommended that you:

Take Immediate Acton To Control the Situation: A case in point is the famous Rodney King incident shown on television several years ago in Los Angels. Of course an investigation was conducted on the application of excessive force; however, supervisors responding to the scene should have taken immediate control to cease and desist any excessive force which was not the case. The investigator may be the ranking officer responding to the scene of an incident. In such case it is your responsibility to take control of the situation and prevent any unnecessary or excessive force. I taught a group of newly promoted supervisors a course on internal investigations, I specifically stated to take control of the situation on no less than five occasion: taking control of the incident. Several weeks later a supervisor taking the class was written up on disciplinary charges for failing to take control of a use of force incident. The supervisor stated that the emergency response team personnel immediately surrounded the inmate and began using force with riot batons, the supervisor could not see what was going on. The inmate complained of gross brutality and the responding supervisor's testimony was that he could not see what was going on. This will not hold up in court, a supervisor cannot take a group of officers in full riot gear including riot batons, stand back and let the officers do whatever they want. That supervisor is responsible to strictly supervise those officers, take complete control, remain in control and terminate the situation as quickly as possible.

Assess quickly the nature and extent of the incident. Interview officer(s) on the scene is usually the first step.

Account for the location of staff as well as determine if any are being held hostage.

Determine if additional personnel are needed

Report via of portable radio the extent of the emergency condition so that the correctional emergency response team (CERT) can dress-out if needed and so that the shift supervisor, chief of security and others will know what is going on. Note: You may pre-establish a different radio frequency to relay the above information so that only the staff and not inmates will hear what is going on.

No investigation can commence if the area is in turmoil. Your first obligation is to insure that the safety, security, and good order of the facility is restored.

Medical Care: Your next obligation is to ensure immediate emergency medical attention is provided to all persons involved staff and inmates. If there is an indication of a use of physical force between a certain officer and an inmate, that officer should not be assigned to escort the inmate to the medical clinic or hospital to prevent a further use of force or allegations from the inmate. In cases where inmates are injured in an altercation among themselves, the inmate with the more serious injuries should be escorted to medical first If both of the inmate's injuries are equally as serious both should be escorted to the medical clinic, with necessary staff assigned to insure that a second altercation does not occur.

Identify Participants: If possible, try to identify participants and witnesses to the incident. Some incidents may involve fights between inmates where none of the inmates involved in the fight can be immediately identified. For example, two inmates start a fight, a group of other inmates surrounds the fighters and by the time that the officers gets through the crowd, the fight has ceased. The first source of information should be the staff assigned to the area at the time of the incident. If the officer reports that he did not witness the fight, he may be able to provide information on tensions between particular inmates, specific troublesome inmates and so on, this will assist you in focusing your investigation.

In some circumstances inmates will not know the names of other inmates assigned to the housing unit. The inmate may be able to identify other inmates by their "street" or jail nicknames or by physical descriptions including scars, tattoos, their room or bed location.

In cases involving the use of physical force there should be a detention center policy in place specific to the jail environment as opposed to what I have witnessed in some rural jails, namely, one policy both for law enforcement and jailers. Correctional officers work under a different set of physical circumstances than police officers working in the community with a possibility of a perpetrator using a firearm against them. Indeed, the federal court has different expectations for correctional officers involved in the use of force. I will go into this area in more detail in chapter 6. Any jail staff that participates in or witnesses a use of force by staff should be required to submit a report in writing. This includes administrative support personnel, medical personnel and visitors. Case in Point: A Catholic nun was walking down the hall of a large detention center. She observed an altercation between an inmate and a officer. The supervisory report of investigation never mentioned the weekly visitor. A follow-up internal affairs investigation requested by the department's Commissioner of Investigations revealed that the nun was present before, during and after the incident. However, the facility investigator's report never mentioned this. When questioned by the internal affairs investigator the nun reported that the officer provoked the incident and slammed the inmate against the wall for no obvious reason before the inmate started resisting and punched the officer. The nun further reported that she would have gladly submitted a report "but nobody asked me". In most cases employees are obligated by policy to submit a report; however, visitors are not required to submit a report to the jail or the investigating officer but a report should be requested and noted in the report of investigation that the eyewitness was present but the visitor refused to submit a report. By identifying the visitor and the circumstances a follow-up investigation by internal affairs or law enforcement may encourage the visitor to relate the facts of the incident.

Notifications: Make notifications as required by policy. It is very embarrassing for a sheriff or jail administrator to receive a telephone inquiry over the weekend from a member of the press who may have responded to the hospital after hearing the call for emergency medical technicians over his police scanner. If the press calls the sheriff at home and asks for details, the sheriff will be highly upset if he has to reply that he does not know anything about it. In a case that I am familiar with an incident occurred early Saturday morning. The press called the sheriff at home and asked for details. The sheriff replied, I am sorry but I have to get back to you. I don't know anything about it. The news reporter responded that it was mind boggling that the sheriff did not know what was going on in his own jail. This embarrassed the sheriff and I am sure that I do not have to tell you what happened when the sheriff is embarrassed by his staff, yes, it rolls down hill.

Preserve the Scene: If required, preserve the scene of the incident, including relevant documents, to wit, log books, suicide observation sheets etc. One of the most important aspects of securing the crime scene is to preserve the scene with minimal contamination and disturbance of any physical evidence by inmates or staff. According to Wrobleski and Hess (1979), every time a crime is committed the perpetrator(s) either brings some evidence to the scene or leaves with some traceable evidence. This area will also be discussed in more detail in chapter 2.

Identification of Witnesses: If your preliminary inquiry does not immediately identify witnesses to an incident, you must take an active stance in searching for witnesses. As previously stated, witnesses include staff, visitors and inmates. If there is a question regarding which staff were present or should have been present review the area logbook. Before making a public announcement in front of all the inmates asking for inmate witnesses, you should ask the reporting officer who was in the area or who might have been in the area. One should never holler out in front of all the inmates that you are looking for witnesses to the incident because you probably will not get one witness. No inmate wishes to be branded as a snitch; therefore, do not question inmate witnesses in front of one another. We will discuss this subject in more detail in chapter 2.

Obtaining Statements & Interviewing Participants and Witnesses: Obtaining statements and interviewing participants and witnesses is one of the most important parts of any investigation. Generally, it is best to question an involved staff member orally first. Asking for a written statement immediately usually puts the officer on the defensive and he/she may be reluctant to give the investigator all the details needed. It is best to separate staff and inmate witnesses to prevent collaboration.

In an inmate-on-inmate altercation, if there is a victim, I usually interview the victim first especially if he/she is awaiting emergency medical transport. A victim may identify his attacker more readily than an uninterested bystander. If the victim is reluctant to speak to you, you can assure the victim that any statements that he makes will not be discussed with any other inmate or staff participant or witness. You may also assure the victim protection by transferring him to another housing unit, transfer to protective custody or to another detention center or by assuring the inmate that his attacker will be transferred to administrative segregation and/or reclassified to special management housing depending upon all the facts and circumstances.

If there is no victim or a victim cannot be identified, the investigator should then speak with witnesses to the incident. If your facility has the capability to continuously record inmate activities on a 24 hour basis, of course the investigator would review the recording and make a copy of the recording for disciplinary proceedings and/or possible prosecution. In cases where inmates refuse to submit written or oral statements investigators should list the inmate's name and other identifying information with a notation they refused to make any oral or written statements or they stated they did not see anything even though they were in a position to witness the incident. This information may be useful in a follow-up investigation by others. Sometimes inmates are reluctant to give written statements to the facility investigator and do not trust them for fear that staff and other inmates will find out information they disclosed; however, they may provide information at a later time to an outside source or a supervisor within the facility that they do trust. You should not make any assumptions about the incident from an inmate's refusal to cooperate. There can be many reasons for the refusal. The inmate may be afraid, may not wish to become involved, may not want to discuss his own misconduct, or may be unwilling to cooperate with anyone in authority.

Investigators should not only conduct oral interviews with staff and inmates but also obtain written statements if possible. I like to begin interviewing immediately upon arrival on the scene, step out of sight for a few moments and jot down in a pocket sized notebook the date, time and statements made. I step out of sight because experience tells me that some people are reluctant to talk when they see you writing down everything they say. After I receive the written statements, guess what? There is usually a significant inconsistency between the oral statement and the written statement that must be addressed.

Ordinarily, the last person that I interview is the alleged perpetrator. The victim and witnesses may provide enough information and evidence to make your case against the suspect, so that you can try to gain a confession based upon the overwhelming evidence.

Interviews: Based upon my experience and success in conducting interviews, I find that interviews should be conducted in private with one person at a time. Inmates should be interviewed in an area where your interview cannot be overheard by other inmates, or in use of force investigations, by any staff involved in the incident. The best place to interview an inmate is out of sight and hearing from other inmates, such as a vacant attorney visitation room, vacant visitation room, empty inmate classroom, general library, and so on. Ideally, the investigating supervisor should conduct interviews with staff members in a private location. The location should be free from unnecessary distraction and out of sight and hearing of any other witnesses or participants. Your employee work rules or handbook should have a statement that employees are required to cooperate in any official agency investigation and that they are required to speak the truth at all times in giving testimony and are not permitted to withhold information. Also, other employees who may not have been identified as witnesses previously cannot elect to stand silent if they have information on a matter under investigation. Review your employee handbook to determine if Garrity Warnings apply before interviewing employees. The Garrity Warnings came about in <u>Garrity v. New Jersey</u> (1972), it is an advisement of the rights usually administered by state or local investigators, or Directors of Human Resources to their employees who may be the target of an internal investigation. It advises the employee of the charge and the administrative liability for any statements made to the investigator. If it does not conflict with the employee handbook, it may also advise employees of their right under the Fifth Amendment to the U.S. Constitution to remain silent on issues that could implicate the employee in a crime.

Preliminary Investigation Outline

As previously defined in this chapter, an investigation is the collection of information to describe and explain an event or series of events; therefore, a preliminary investigation consist of the actions performed by the investigator immediately upon responding to the scene of a crime and/or unusual occurrence. Wrobleski and Hess (1979) formulated an investigative process outline below that I have had tremendous success with. When I teach law enforcement detectives they are extremely impressed with this outline and find it very user friendly and workable. It will assist the internal investigator no matter what type of incident under inquiry. This process outline may also be used to structure your investigation. The investigator must obtain answers to the questions: Who? What? Where? When? How? Why? And what actions taken?

Who? Are suspects?

Are accomplices?
Were the victims?
Were the associates?
Was interviewed?
Were eyewitnesses?
Saw or heard something important?
Reported the incident?
Made the complaint?
Marked and received evidence?
Was notified?
Had a motive?

What? Type of crime or unusual occurrence was committed?

Was the approximate amount of damage to property?
Happened (narrative of the actions of suspect, victims, and witnesses?
Evidence was found?
Preventive measures had been taken?
Knowledge, skill or strength was needed?
Was said?
Further information is needed?
Further action is needed?

When? Did the incident occur?

Was it discovered?
Was it reported?

Where? Did the incident occur?

Was evidence found?
Was evidence stored?
Are victims, witnesses and suspects located or housed?

How? Was the incident discovered?

> Does the incident relate to others?
> Did the incident occur?
> Was evidence found?
> Was information obtained?

Why? Was the offense/crime committed?

> Was certain property stolen?
> Was a particular time selected?

What Actions Taken (Investigator): The investigator should list actions taken (e.g. reviewed 24 hour recording of inmate housing unit etc.)

Note Taking

One should take notes from the beginning to the conclusion of an investigation. Almost everything that you learn should be reduced to writing. I recommend that investigators carry a small writing pad in their pocket. Write down the events and oral testimony related to you even if you do not think it has relevancy at that time, you may change your mind as the facts develop. The more complete one's notes are, the less time one will waste later trying to repeat parts of the investigation, remember who said what or try to remember different aspects. Write down your own thoughts as you go including additional areas to pursue. If you have an idea or a question to ask or a lead to pursue, so as not to forget it, write it down. Do not hesitate to take photographs and make sketches as they will help describe an incident far more readily than hundreds of words.

References

Guidelines for the development of policies & procedures. (August 1991) Adult Correctional Institutions. American Correctional Association, Laurel,MD pp. 185- 186.

Aboud, A. (1986). <u>Investigations manual</u>. Labor Relations Alternative, Inc. Produced with a grant from the New York State Governor's Office of Employee Relations.

Bernstein, M.A. (1997). <u>Evidence - a modern application of dying declaration exception</u> to hearsay rule. Suffolk University Law Review 30 (Summer) 575-81.

<u>Canons of Police Ethics</u> (1956). Preservation of Evidence, Christian Police and Prison Association. CPAUSA/aol.com Retrieved 2014, 12, 01.

Fisher v. Koehler, 83 Civ., 2128, (MEL), (1987).

Garrity v. New Jersey, 385 U.S. 493 (1967).

Gifis, S.H. (1984) <u>Law Dictionary</u>. Woodbury, N.Y.: Barrons Educational Series, Inc.

Hamilton v. Love, 328 F. Supp. 1182 (E.D.) (Ark. 1971).

Hess, K.M.& Orthmann, C.H. (2010). <u>Criminal investigation</u>. (9th ed.). Delmar Cengage Learning, Clifton Park, N.Y.

U.S. v. Terrell County, Ga. 457 F. Supp. 2d 1359 (M.D. Ga 2006).

Wrobleski, H. & Hess, K.M. (1979). <u>Introduction to law enforcement and criminal justice</u>. New York: West Publishing Co.

Chapter 2

RESPONSIBILITIES OF THE INVESTIGATING OFFICER

Chapter Learning Objectives

- Identify the major responsibilities of the investigating officer
- Explain how to establish and protect the crime scene
- Summarize the importance of searching for contraband
- Discuss the guidelines for inmate and staff interviews
- Discuss the guidelines for interviewing techniques
- Define spontaneous declarations
- Explain the factors involved in accepting a confession
- Establish reliability of inmate informants

Major Responsibility of Investigating Officer

After taking control of the emergency as discussed in Chapter 1, the investigator should secure the crime scene, videotape, photograph, take notes, sketch, search for contraband, recover evidence, obtain statements from all concerned, identify possible suspects and present an objective analysis of all the facts and circumstances. Photographs and video tape accurately portray the crime scene for disciplinary investigations, criminal prosecution and so on. Since probe teams and correctional emergency response teams usually respond with a video camera, the investigator may be able to film the incident while it is in progress and/or identify possible witnesses and suspects who may later claim that they were never present at the incident. This author respectfully recommends taking an overall view of the entire area then zooming in on particular evidentiary scenes. Video tape or photograph possible weapons wherever discovered, inmates with blood on their clothing, inmates with possible injuries and so on. The investigator can later place photographs and video recordings on compact disc to be submitted with the investigative report. This is especially true of large correctional institutions that have the capability of 24-hour recording of inmate housing units and activities areas.

After gathering of all the facts and evidence you may wish to submit with your report a sketch to assist the reviewer (warden or deputy warden) in visualizing the crime scene, location of evidence, location of possible perpetrators and/or witnesses. Sketches can relay the actual location of objects and evidence and possible witnesses to an incident While investigating an inmate allegation of excessive force, an inmate eyewitness reported to this writer that he observed the entire incident from his cell. I drew a sketch to show that the inmate's reported exact location was impossible for the inmate to view what he reported. Sometimes reviewing authorities have questions in their minds that require an answer, a sketch should clear up any possible questions of the reviewer. A good sketch should show measured distances and a scale, i.e. weapon found six inches from the entrance of the housing unit as if the perpetrator or possible accomplice tried to discard it. Remember the old adage, *"a picture is worth a thousand words".*

The investigator should visually scan the entire area to thoroughly assess the scene and note any possible secondary crime scene. Note any objects (weapons, suicide notes etc.). Document your observations, including the location of persons and items within the crime scene and the appearance of and condition of the scene upon arrival. Take photographs of the area and supplement by drawing sketches. Include such information as lights on/off, door opened/closed, smells (marijuana, smoke), etc. Also document any spontaneous declarations (utterances) made by staff, victim or witnesses, and any made direct or overheard. Include any out of the ordinary behavior observed, i.e. possible suspects hyperventilating, out of breath and so forth.

The facility investigator may have to assist law enforcement personnel in conducting their official inquiry and the medical examiner/coroner prior to conducting the facility internal investigation. At the conclusion of the outside investigations then the facility investigator can begin his/her investigation and hopefully the outside investigator's will share the information that they have. The outside investigators may or may not share their findings and conclusions with the internal investigator. Whatever information you can obtain from them should be dated and documented for your report. It has been my experience that some Sheriffs may assign a law enforcement detective investigator and not use the facility investigator. Also, do not be surprised if the Sheriff requests an investigator from the State Police so as to show objectivity and no cover-up.

The investigator should photograph evidence using a still camera. Be prepared to reproduce several photographs, that is, one copy for any reports leaving the command going to central office, law enforcement, board of correction, and facility file. If law enforcement becomes involved they will usually take their own photographs

Establish The Crime Scene

One of the most important aspects of securing the scene is to preserve the scene with minimal contamination and disturbance of any physical evidence. The first responder to the scene should be highly observant and should not handle anything unless it appears to be an apparent inmate suicide. Of course the officer should lift the inmate's legs up so that the hangman's noose is not making tension around the neck while another officer cuts the noose and lays the inmate flat on the floor awaiting the arrival of emergency medical personnel. Inmate suicides will be discussed in detail in Chapter 9. An apparent inmate suicide should be treated as a possible homicide until cleared as a suicide by the medical examiner/coroner or law enforcement officials.

If the shift supervisor has not already established boundaries of the scene, the investigating officer should. Starting at the focal point and extending outward include the location of the crime, the most reasonable points of exit and entry of possible perpetrators, suspects and witnesses. Establish physical barriers using crime scene tape or rope. Take measures to protect any evidence that may be available including photographing, sketching, moving or confiscating and placing in an evidence bag.

Remove all persons from the area and assign an officer with a logbook to make sure no one visits the crime scene that does not have a legitimate need to be there. As previously stated, the officer should record everyone who visits the scene, their name, title, agency (if outside agency), reason for visiting the scene, date and time of arrival and departure. Forensic investigators may not wish persons who visit the scene to smoke, chew tobacco, eat, drink, adjust thermostat or open any windows or doors, touch anything unnecessarily, reposition any moved items, litter, or spit within the established boundaries of the crime scene unless approved to do so by law enforcement personnel or the medical examiner.

The officer posted on the scene should be cautioned not to touch anything unnecessarily, reposition any items, remove any litter, and refrain from cleaning within the boundaries of the scene. The assigned officer should have absolute authority at the scene until the arrival of the warden, designee, law enforcement personnel or medical examiner. The assigned officer should document the original location of the victim and objects that have been observed and/or relocated. If, for any reason, the assigned correctional officer determines that an employee does not have an official need to enter the crime scene, access should be denied unless permission is granted from the shift supervisor, higher ranking supervisor manager or the investigating officer. Oftentimes fellow officers wish to visit the scene and look around but the scene should never be contaminated by people who do not have a legitimate need to be there.

The Chief of Security or designee should ensure equipment is available for the establishment and search of a crime scene. Adams, Caddell & Knutsinger (2004), suggest the following essential items for a crime scene kit. The list is not presented in sequential order of importance:

- Crime scene barrier tape or rope
- Digital camera
- Evidence log
- Crime scene log
- Personal protective equipment such as biohazard latex gloves
- Heavy duty rubber gloves and masks
- Two-way radio or landline telephone or issue facility cell phone
- Evidence bags and paper bags
- Video recording camera
- Flashlight and extra batteries
- First aid kit
- Ruler, paper clips for fastening items
- Privacy screen (if deemed necessary)
- Search mirrors
- Metal detectors
- Physical plant diagrams
- Incident reporting forms and spiral bound notebook
- Measuring tape (or rolling measuring device)
- Clipboard
- Magnets for retrieving small metal objects from hard to reach places
- Tweezers (grabbing device)
- Magnifying glass for close-up examination of possible evidence

Search for Contraband

For investigative purposes a search should be conducted to recover missing or stolen property, to prevent disturbances, to recover evidence such as weapons, drugs, evidence of sexual assault such as clothing, underwear, or sheets. A Search should be conducted to recover escape tools and to ensure the safety and security of the institution especially after a disturbance when there may be a reasonable belief that detection and recovery of physical evidence is necessary. Most facility policies and procedures require that searches be conducted in a way to avoid unnecessary use of physical force or destruction of inmate property. The U.S. Appeals Court in McCray v. State of Maryland (1972) ruled that strip searches shall be conducted with maximum courtesy and respect for the inmate's dignity and with minimal physical discomfort and embarrassment.

Correctional staff should be trained in conducting cell searches, dormitory searches, pat frisk, strip searches and so on and under what conditions searches should be conducted. Staff should also be trained at the academy on who can conduct body cavity searches and under what conditions; therefore, I will not belabor this issue. A housing area search may be authorized by the investigating officer as previously stated to recover contraband, to detect possible DNA evidence on clothing or escape related paraphernalia. A general area search namely, classrooms, workshop and other non-living areas of the facility should be conducted when the incident occurs therein or a possible perpetrator re-enters the general area after committing a crime or serious rule violation depending on the facts and circumstances. Perimeter search and inspection should be conducted in cases where inmate possible perpetrators work outside the secure perimeter to recover weapons or for possible attempted escapes or escape related activity. An inmate informed this author while supervising a housing area search that, *"if an inmate wants to hide something they will hide it right in front of the officer's face".* Indeed, the inmate had a roach (Marijuana butt) hidden in a garbage bag inside his cell that the officer poured out on the floor but failed to closely analyze the contents.

There is no *"unlawful search and seizure"* (Fourth Amendment freedom from unreasonable searches and seizure) of inmates with reasonable suspicion that they may be concealing contraband or related to legitimate penal interests of safety, security and good order. Also, courts have held that where a genuine emergency exists, officials may be more restrictive than they otherwise may be and certain services may also be temporarily suspended without violating the constitution (Eighth Amendment). This includes lock-down of inmates during or directly after a major disturbance for an investigation (Waring v. Meachum, 2001).

According to Bennett and Hess (2001), the search of the crime scene locates, identifies and preserves any evidence that is present. It may also identify the perpetrator and show how a crime was committed. The type of crime will determine the type of evidence that officers and investigators should be looking for.

When conducting searches for drugs the investigator can contact their local law enforcement agency that is, police, sheriff, or U.S. Customs personnel unless the facility maintains their own drug finding canines. Since there are numerous places to secret drugs in a correctional facility, canines should be ideal. While supervising a search in a large county jail, I observed U.S. Customs canines at work. The inmates formed a straight line and walked past a canine. When an inmate had a small amount of Marijuana (half a cigarette/joint) on him, the dog sat down right in front of the inmate thus signaling the inmate was in possession of a quantity of a controlled substance. A strip search of the inmate validated the canine's actions. The use of canines can make a search of a large area go very quickly; however, you must be prepared to have inmate linens exchanged in that some canines may stand on the bed to sniff or slobber on the inmate's linen. At this same detention center I also observed canines walk past an employee's car with the doors and windows closed and locked and go to the sitting position informing the handler that drugs was in fact present in the vehicle.

Investigators should not jump from one area of a crime scene to another instead carry out a methodical and systematic search as follows: Point-to-Point search - the investigator enters the crime scene from the point of entrance and approaches the first item of what may be considered evidence. After properly securing the evidence, the investigator then goes to the next closest item and secures it. The above process should be repeated until the room or area has been systematically and carefully scrutinized. Sector Search - in New York City, police precincts are divided into sectors; therefore, sub-divide the large correctional facility into rooms or floors, institution's roof, ground area outside of facility and so on. Each employee is then assigned to a specific search area reporting to a sector supervisor. Upon discovering an item of evidence, the officer assisting the investigator should be instructed to continue searching for any additional evidence that may be recovered.

I observed something that truly amazed me at that time having twenty-five years in corrections. I observed a chief of security conducting a search in a rural Mississippi jail. The officers appeared to have conducted a thorough search of a housing unit and discovered the expected amount of usual contraband. What amazed this writer was the chief selected a different group of officers and told them to search the same housing unit again although he was not looking for anything in particular. The newly selected staff looked puzzled because everyone could see that the area had been thoroughly searched already. To everyone's amazement at the conclusion of the second search the officers recovered more contraband than was discovered by the first group.

Conducting Inmate/Staff Interviews

The Connecticut Department of Corrections, Center for Training and Staff Development defines an interview as a tool used to gain information about the facts and circumstances surrounding an event (unusual occurrence). It is face-to-face questioning and response between supervisor and subject regarding an event that is of official interest to the correctional institution based upon facility policy and procedures. The most important source of information in an investigation is the testimony of an eyewitness (also ear witness) to the event. All persons who are suspected of being a participant or witness to an incident under investigation should be interviewed. With staff interviews in some states the supervisor must provide Garrity Warnings as previously discussed. Just as the Miranda Warnings ensures the inmate's constitutional rights, so does the Garrity Warnings ensure the employee's constitutional rights which will preserve the evidentiary value of any statements the employee may make. If an inmate is a target of an investigation to which he will be arrested, Miranda Warnings must be given prior to the investigator interrogating the inmate.

As stated above, before interrogating a suspect in custody, the investigator must give the individual Miranda Warnings as required by Miranda v. Arizona(1966). The target of the investigation, namely, the inmate suspect must be informed of his right to remain silent, to have an attorney present at any time during the questioning, if the inmate cannot afford an attorney a court appointed attorney will be provided. The inmate must be warned that anything they say may be used against them in a court of law. It is advisable to have the warnings listed on a card and read them to the suspect. If you do it from memory it could damage the case at trial if a defense attorney ask you to repeat the warnings you gave to his client and being nervous on the stand you leave out some critical information to which the attorney will probably say that the investigating officer failed to inform the inmate of his rights. If your read it to him, all one has to do is take out your card and read the card to the court. After each warning ask the suspect if he understands each of the rights that you read and if necessary clarified to him and state whether or not the inmate agreed to waive his rights and answer your questions. If the inmate avails himself to his constitutional rights to have an attorney present during the interrogation the questioning must cease and desist at that time. It is important that you state in your written report that the inmate was provided Miranda Warnings prior to the interrogation.

In some cases inmate witnesses may not provide statements to detention center investigators because they realize that facility investigators are also staff and supervisors. The inmate may feel that it will not be a fair and impartial investigation because employees ride to work together, hang-out together and so forth; therefore, investigators will try to cover their staff regardless of the truth. In some cases a higher ranking supervisory investigator at the rank of Chief of Security, Associate Warden or Deputy Warden may be able to obtain inmate statements or a supervisor that has a reputation of fundamental fairness, one who they believe is on the side of "right" no matter who is involved, one who will "let the chips fall where they may".

If the inmate is transferred to a state prison, the investigating officer may be able to contact the receiving prison investigations unit and have the receiving institution interview the inmate and obtain a written statement to be faxed to the transferring facility.

It cannot be said enough, that the investigator must separate all inmate and staff participants and witnesses from one another to avoid discussion of the incident and concocting similar stories to cover one another. Early on in my tenure in corrections I observed staff and inmates being allowed to sit at a table, discuss the incident and write statements in agreement with one another. Each individual should be interviewed out of sight and hearing of all other participants and witnesses. I begin the interview by identifying myself if they don't know me, I call their attention to the date and time of the incident and ask them if they were present, where they were, and what they saw and heard. As previously stated in Chapter 1, all of my questions are formulated to answer the questions: who, what, when, where, how, why and what actions, if any taken. I elicit only the facts, not assumptions, hearsay or personal opinions.

Interviewing Techniques

Interview: Webster's II New College Dictionary (2005) defines an interview as a formal face-to-face meeting conducted by the interviewer in which information is elicited. The national expert on interviewing and interrogation and consultant to the Federal Bureau of Investigation on interviewing and interrogation, is John Reid, Reid College of Interviewing and Interrogations. I attended the Reid course and found it to be an outstanding course that I was able to apply immediately in a variety of situations. According to Reid (1988), and interview is the questioning of people who are perceived to possess knowledge of activities that may be of interest to the investigator.

Interrogation: Interrogation differs from an interview, this is a term used to describe the process by which suspects are rigorously questioned by the interrogator, guilt is probable, and must be preceded by Miranda Warnings (Gifis 1984). According to Reid (1988) an interrogation is an art of questioning and observation, the truth is elicited from a suspect by sound reasoning and understanding without the use of threats or promises. Guilt should be reasonably suspected in that interrogation is accusatory.

Prior to conducting a scheduled interview I usually make a checklist so that all of the significant points that I need to cover are accomplished. No matter what the unusual occurrence is, I never speak in a disrespectful manner to the suspect or give him the impression that I loathe or disrespect him based on the fact the he is an inmate or the incident under investigation. An inmate suspect will not provide you with any information if you talk down to him or speak in a manner that makes the inmate feel that you are disgusted with him or actions he may be accused of. And, of course you should never use insulting language or speak as if you are smarter than the inmate.

Case in Point I: I observed an interview between a facility investigator and an inmate shortly after a correctional officer reported that he was first assaulted by the inmate prior to using physical force in self defense. The investigator spoke to the inmate as if he had already formed a conclusion that the inmate was guilty and constantly looked at his watch and out the window. To my surprise, the inmate said, *"why am I talking to you, you've already made up your mind what happened and you are not going to believe anything I say because all you want to do is cover your staff. You are more concerned with beating the traffic on your way home"*.

Case in Point II: Prior to being transferred to state prison a serial rapist grew a thick mustache, shaved his head and transferred from protective custody to general population because he did not wish to go to prison and be on lock-down for 23 hours in protective custody for sexual abuse of children. He hoped that no one would find out about his charges; therefore, he could remain in prison general population. Before transfer to prison he was sexually assaulted with a large rough commercial wooden toilet brush by a relative of one of the 15 year old girls that he was convicted of raping. Prior to the victim being transported to the hospital he named his assailant and the other inmates who held him down. Upon interrogating the suspect I read the Miranda Warnings and I was cordial polite and sensitive to the personal concerns of the suspect with sincere eye contact. In brief, I provided a possible moral justification for his action (revenge for a relative) not a legal justification. According to Reid (1988) the investigator cannot expect a person to confess without giving him the opportunity to couple his admission with an excuse that allows him to save his self respect. I informed the inmate of the evidence against him and I allowed him to give a complete account of the incident without interrupting him. After he completed his statement I went back and asked questions and probed deeper into certain areas while observing his non-verbal behavior to questions I asked him. As stated above, I provided a possible moral justification for his actions to observe his non-verbal behavior as follows: "was it because you were exacting punishment on the rapist for raping so many children? The inmate feeling that he had someone before him that understands confessed and reported, *"I wanted to show him how a 15 year old virgin feels when she is forced and has sex for the first time in her life".* Frankly I did not care about his moral justification I wanted a confession for possible prosecution and I got it. Conscientious investigators should consider requesting their agency send them to the John Reid College of Interviewing and Interrogation, it is the absolute best training you could ever receive, believe me their methods work. It is not a lot of useless philosophy instead it is practical tactics and techniques that you can apply to almost any situation and you will gain the confidence you need to become an outstanding investigator able to read truthful and deceptive individuals and learn the techniques for gaining a confession.

When I interview or interrogate anyone I never have barriers between the interviewer and interviewee as shown on most television programs. Television programs show the detective sitting at a table with the suspect sitting in front of him. The interviewer cannot observe the individuals body language to see the impact that various questions may have on the suspect. I respectfully recommend a book by Nierenburg & Calero (1971), *"How to Read a Person Like a Book".* This book is an excellent introduction to reading body language by viewing individuals' various body positions and involuntary body movements with an explanation of what their body language is communicating. A more contemporary work is by the legendary behaviorist David J. Lieberman, *"You Can Read Anyone"* (2007). Both books can be purchased very inexpensively in paperback on Amazon.com. The suspect's body language may be just as important or even more important than the words coming out of their mouths. Applied as instructed, investigators can even read family members for truth and deception, I have and gained confessions of family prohibited behavior.

Investigators should beware of statements that inmates have rehearsed. They are willing to repeat it verbatim over and over again. If the individual is being truthful the facts will remain the same but will change slightly each time that he/she repeats the statements. Hess and Orthmann (2010), recommends that after an individual has informed the investigator as to what occurred, guide the interview to some other aspect of the incident. Later return to the topic and ask the person to repeat the story. Of course the authors recommend using open relaxed posture, facing the subject but not staring, make eye contact and occasionally say "okay".

If you are a fan of the television program Judge Judy, you will notice she always says: *"Don't look down at the floor, look directly at me"*! Experts on interviewing and interrogation say that *"the eyes are the windows of the soul"* A trained individual can tell if one is being truthful or deceptive by several different means. For example, prior to my asking an interviewee a question we both had good eye contact, but after I asked a particular question about the incident the interviewee suddenly breaks eye contact and does not want to look at me. This puts the investigator on notice that they should further probe a particular line of inquiry because the interviewee is uncomfortable with that line of questioning. Also, if I ask a particular question about the incident and before answering the interviewee takes off his glasses and examines the glasses for a second or two when nothing is wrong with the glasses. This tells me that he is pondering his reply to my question before answering he is trying to figure out just how much do I know about his involvement and how much should he say because he does not wish to get caught up in a lie.

Spontaneous Declarations

According to Black's Law Dictionary (1999), in the law of evidence, an excited utterance is an unplanned reaction to a startling event. It is a statement made by a person in response to a startling or shocking event or condition and it is an exception to the hearsay rule and is admissible to prove the truth of the statement itself (p. 585). According to Gifis (1984), spontaneous exclamations made by participants victims, or witnesses to an incident (or crime) immediately before, during or after the incident in evidence such written or oral statements as excited utterances are admissible (p. 406). Many states have also adopted the federal rules of evidence patterned after federal rules. According to the Federal

Rules of Evidence spontaneous statements are statements made by suspected perpetrators, witnesses or victims close to the point of time to the event who may be startled by the event and before they have had an opportunity to reflect on the events reported. The investigator should note exactly what was said by the various participants and observers at the time of the incident or immediately thereafter. Often those involved will change their accounts of the incident after they have had an opportunity to converse with jail house lawyers, gang members and others.

The investigator should quote the spontaneous statements with date, time and location and any witnesses who also heard the statements. After receiving the written report the investigator should compare the spontaneous statement with the written report received and resolve any inconsistencies. To summarize Article VIII, Rule 803, of the Federal Rules of Evidence, investigators are not under any legal obligation to stop the person making the excited utterances and advice him of his 5th Amendment rights of silence. Indeed, the investigator is simply listening to volunteered incriminating utterances and Miranda Warnings do not have to be given for unsolicited spontaneous statements or confessions.

Confessions

You may ponder the question, once I have received a spontaneous declaration that amounts to a confession or, I receive a confession after an interview that the investigation is pretty much over. Quite the contrary, once the investigator obtains a confession one must immediately begin checking the details of the confession and corroborate the information contained in the confession. According to the Federal Rules of Evidence regarding confessions, *"It is a statement by the accused which tends to support the charge, but which is not sufficient to determine guilt, the confession must have been corroborated"* (Section 801). The investigator must introduce independent evidence which will establish the validity of the confession. One can see the obvious reasons why a confession must be corroborated. Working in a detention facility or prison there are a number of so-called inmate power brokers whom other inmates fear for a variety of reasons. It is quite possible that an inmate bully may order a fearful and/or weaker inmate to confess to a rule violation that the bully committed so that the bully will get off the hook.

Case in Point: In the Son of Sam serial murders in New York City in the 1970s, prior to the capture of the Son of Sam, television news programs reported that there were a number of individuals, some suffering from mental illness and some pranksters who called police and voluntarily reported and confessed that they were in fact the Son of Sam serial killer. Police had the monumental task of corroborating the volunteered confessions only to find out that all who voluntarily confessed were not the real Son of Sam and had no involvement in the murders.

According to Royal and Schutt (1976), confessions are generally admissible, even though they are:

- Gained through trickery or deceit (so long as the trickery or deceit does not shock the conscience of the community). For example, if the investigator borrows his brother's clergy clothing and allows the inmate to confess to whom the inmate thinks is a priest who will not divulge privileged information. Then the investigator returns and says, "aha, I have your confession right here". This would shock the conscience of the community.
- Not in writing
- Unsigned
- Not made under oath
- Made without benefit of advice of legal counsel

In most cases, suspects do not know who may have provided information to the investigator this includes inmate snitches and staff informants who may have provided damaging information on the suspect. Additionally, with the television program CSI (Crime Scene Investigation) inmate suspects may not know if the investigator actually has the forensic resources and ability to have obtained the evidence (fingerprints, DNA, etc.) as the investigator informs the inmate that he has in his possession; therefore, the investigator may gain a confession on presentation of the fabricated evidence. Or, the inmate may confess to mitigate his involvement with others.

According to Moffa, (2008) some television programs may overestimate the reliability of forensic evidence; therefore, investigators should be trained (John Reid College of Interviewing and Interrogation) on the technique of gaining confessions through trickery and deceit. Simply stated, convincing the inmate suspect that the investigator has evidence (fabricated evidence) that does not really exist. When the investigator presents this fabricated evidence and you see the inmate break eye contact, delay in answering your question while he scratches his head, starts wringing his hands and looking around the room, he is very much so considering that you do in fact have the evidence you so state.

Case in Point: During an investigation of excessive force on an inmate who obtained substantial injuries, I witnessed an internal affairs investigator interviewing the officer who was alleged by the inmate to have brutally committed an assault and battery upon his person with a side-handled baton (PR 24) as the inmate stated he lay defenseless on the floor begging the officer to stop. The officer accused refused to change his oral testimony or his written report. The investigator fabricated evidence as follows. Upon a signal from the interviewer another investigator walked over to the interviewer and laid a folder on his desk, he looked at the officer and walked out of the room. The interviewer took a moment to open the folder pretended that he was reading some reports, closed the folder, looked out the window for a few seconds, smiled and then said to the officer. *"Are you going to stick to that story or tell the truth, I have several staff witnesses' reports threatened with disciplinary action for lying, have submitted addendums to their reports saying that the incident happened just as reported by the inmate. So I have no further questions for you at this time, I am going to turn this over to the District Attorney's office".* The officer's face flushed red, looked pale and asked the interviewer, *"sir will you give me a chance to really tell you what happened"?*

The interviewer informed the officer that he could leave. The officer panicked and made a complete confession begging to avoid prosecution. When in fact no staff witness had changed their report as they all supported the officer's account of the incident.

The use of inmate confessions for internal correctional purposes (e.g. disciplinary hearings, classification hearings etc.) is significantly different than a confession that must survive the test of the courts. Generally speaking if the investigator obtains a confession for administrative purposes it should be admissible so long as it can be shown that there is independent evidence to corroborate the confession not obtained by harmful consequences, no undue psychological influences, no promise of reward, that the confession was voluntary, and that the confessor was not impaired due to intoxication or apparent mental illness.

Investigators must be careful when receiving confessions that may wind up in court. If a confession is used in court it will be under careful scrutiny by the defense attorney. Suspects have the right to waive the Miranda Warnings; however, if waived, the investigator must show that the confession was knowing, voluntary, and intelligent (Colorado v. Connelly, (1966). Also, was the suspect's judgment impaired and cast doubt on the confession (Moffa 2008)? Indeed, according to Moffa (2008), although intoxication is not a defense to a crime it cannot be cause for exclusion of the confession. It calls into question the validity and the reliability of the confession and the validity of the suspect's waiver of Miranda Warnings. It is a well known fact that inmates make homemade intoxicants (referred to as Hooch) also inmates may enter the facility having ingested narcotics or withdrawing from narcotics or they may have sources among staff to traffic and secret narcotics to them. A sharp attorney will surely raise these issues. Moffa (2008) also reports that comprehensive findings suggest that both juveniles and adult suspects with low intelligence quotients may not understand the implications of waiving their rights.

Establish Reliability of Inmate Informants

The inmate information network within a facility serves as an invaluable source of communication as to what is going on in the facility. Who is planning to escape? Who is having narcotics brought into the facility and how? Who are the extortionist? These are just some of the questions that individuals responsible for security within the institution wish to know. Answers to the above questions may be provided by inmate informants depending on the reputation of the Chief of Security or similar title. Informants have provided this author with valuable information over the years while investigating unusual occurrences and to prevent incidents. For example, while serving as Chief of Security a confidential inmate informant provided this writer with information of an inmate escape plan in maximum security which turned out to be valid. Although there were many disbelievers at first among supervisors and managers due to the quality of officers and supervisors assigned to the unit and the quality and amount of security cameras in the unit monitored by the control center. Relying upon the informant's information, I supervised two searches of the unit one right after the other and a fully loaded twenty-five automatic pistol was recovered. Also, the rear door hinges were cut leading to the outdoor recreation yard. The escape plan was prevented because of the reliable information provided by the inmate informant.

As chief of security and as a facility investigator I actively recruited inmate confidential informants, especially if an inmate believes that I have went above and beyond the call of duty to help him in the past. I provided a way for inmates to come talk to me without anyone getting suspicious, staff or other inmates with the assistance of the Health Services Administrator through the medical clinic. Inmates may volunteer information to investigators even unsolicited if investigators show that they can be trusted not to divulge the confidential information to line staff who may go back and discuss it in hearing of other inmates or staff that the inmates may not trust as being too friendly with inmates. I do not refer to the inmate's name when discussing confidential information unless I am in a private area with my superiors. I usually refer to informants by a special code name that I create for each one so if I am overheard discussing information no inmate worker or staff will know who I am referring to. I will not belabor herein the serious reprisals to an informant for divulging information to the administration. There is a substantial security interest in keeping the inmate safe.

When I use a confidential inmate informant I must first establish reliability as follows:

- If the inmate has provided reliable documented information in the past in the discovery of and/or prevention of crimes or threats to the safety, security and good order of the facility then I use his present statements as reasonable cause to believe his present statements are probability true also and I state this in my report.
- The informant must state how he has come to possess knowledge of the information that he is relaying to the investigator, to wit, eye or ear witness and under what circumstances?
- In determining the reliability of the informant there must be some independent evidence to corroborate the claims of the confidential informant?
- Does the inmate have substantial self-interest in being perceived as helpful to the administration?

In <u>Reed v. Oregon State Penitentiary</u> (1989) the State Appeals Court ruled that hearing officers must establish reliability of the confidential informant and of the facts supporting the conclusion. Some state appeals court have required that hearing officers dealing with inmate informants' statements must determine whether an informant is a person who is reliable and determine whether the information provided is truthful. In regard to <u>Baker v. Lyles,</u> (1990), the state appeals court of Maryland ruled that an inmate's due process rights were not violated when the disciplinary hearing board convicted him of possession of escape contraband based upon undocumented hearsay of an anonymous inmate informant, under the applicable "some evidence" standard, in view of additional evidence available at the time of the final decision by the warden that the inmate had previously escaped from prison, that abundant work had been done to attain escape through an exhaust fan in the facility's chapel, and that escape tools had been redeemed in prison. Due process requires that a record of disciplinary proceedings document some good faith investigation and findings as to the credibility of confidential inmate informants and the reliability of information provided by them (Williams v. Fountain, 1996).

REFERENCES

Adams, T.E. Caddell, A.C. & Krupsinger (2004). Crime scene investigation, (2nd ed.) New Jersey, Prentice Hall.

Baker v. Lyles, 904 F. 2d 925 (eth Cir. 1990).

Bennett, W.W. & Hess, K.M. (2001). Criminal investigation (6th ed.). Belmont,CA. Wadsworth/Thompson Learning.

Colorado v. Connelly, 479 U.S. 157 (1986).

Dienstein W. (1975). How to write a narrative investigation report. Springfield, IL: Charles C. Thomas Publishing.

Federal Rules of Evidence, Section 1.12, and Section 803 Exceptions Against the Rule of Hearsay United States Courts and Magistrates, 1982.

Garner, B. A. (Ed.) (1990). Blacks law dictionary. (7th ed.) West Group

Garrity v. New Jersey 385 U.S. 493 (1967)

Gifis, S. H. (1984). Law dictionary. Woodbury, N.Y.: Barrons Educational Series, Inc.

Hess, K. M. & Orthmann, C. H. (2010). <u>Criminal investigation</u> (9th ed.). Clifton Park, N.Y. Delmar Cengage Learning

Lieberman, David J. Ph.D. (2007) <u>You can read anyone</u>. New Jersey: Viter Press

McCray v. State of Maryland, 456 F. 2d. (4th Cir. 1972).

Miranda v. Arizona, 384 U.S. 436, (1966).

Moffa, M. S. <u>The evidence and the expert: judgments of their relative importance in confession adjudication</u>. (2008). Psychology Thesis Paper I, httpikdous.rwu.edu/Psych_thesis/-Retrieved 2014, 12-05.

Nierenburg, G. & Calero, H., (1971). <u>How to read a person like a book</u>. Cornerstone

Reed v. Oregon State Penitentiary, 773 F. 2d 5 (OR. App. 1989).

Reid, J.E. (1986). <u>The Reid technique of interviewing and interrogation</u>. John E. reid and Associates, Chicago, Illinois.

Royal, F. & Schutt, S. R. (1976). <u>The gentle art of interviewing and interrogation</u>. N.J. Prentice Hall, Inc.

Waring v. Meachum, 175 F. Supp. 2d 230 (D. Conn. 2001).

<u>Webster's II New College Dictionary</u>. (2005), (3rd ed.) Boston, MA. Houghton Mifflin

Williams v. Fountain, 77 F. 3d 372 (11th Cir. 1996).

Chapter 3

U.S. DISTRICT COURT, SOUTHERN DISTRICT OF NEW YORK

Deficiencies in Facility Internal Investigations

Chapter Learning Objectives

- Explain the importance of documenting unusual occurrences
- List and discuss U.S. Federal Court findings of common deficiencies of internal investigations
- Recognize the common investigation deficiencies in the given case studies

---

The Importance of Documenting Unusual Occurrences

Why bother to report unusual occurrences, conduct internal investigations or discipline inmate offenders or staff? The U.S. District Court, Southern District of New York submits that *"if it is not documented, it never happened"*. When an inmate allegation is made and the correctional agency does not have a paper trail documenting unusual occurrences, investigation of same, possible disciplinary disposition, and a remedy to prevent the incident from happening again then it is an inmate lawsuit waiting to happen. The agency may find itself losing the case in civil court and paying off the inmate and his lawyer.

Case in Pont: An incident occurred at a large detention center in the northeastern United States involving an inmate and a supervisor at the rank of captain. The inmate reported to his attorney and to the attending emergency room physician that the captain assaulted him because he cursed the supervisor. The hospital documented various bruises, contusions and other non-serious injuries sustained by the inmate. Upon returning to the detention center no inmate disciplinary report, no use of force report and no investigation was conducted to validate a use of force or invalidate an inmate allegation of unnecessary force. Indeed, the accused supervisor went home as if nothing had occurred. Also, it was if the incident never occurred in the eyes of the facility administration up until the warden was served with a lawsuit for unnecessary and excessive force. Having no documentation or prior knowledge of any such incident the warden requested that the internal affairs unit conduct an investigation into the matter under litigation.

The findings and conclusions of the internal investigation revealed that the supervisor was verbally provoked in front of several officers and inmates; therefore, the supervisor struck the inmate several times with clenched fist and stomped the inmate at least twice. Facility medical personnel sent the inmate to an outside hospital for treatment and X-rays. Because no reports were written after the incident, no investigation into a use of force was done and no documentation to prove the inmate allegation as untruthful, it was in the best interest of the detention center to make a financial settlement with the inmate. The inmate reported that he did not do anything other than curse at the supervisor and of course we all know that correctional case law states that no amount of verbal provocation justifies a use of physical force by staff. The inmate reported that he did not do anything else to the supervisor. Although the supervisor reported that the inmate came towards him in a threatening manner to assault him, where was the disciplinary report stating that the inmate did anything at all (no violation of any inmate rules of discipline). Of course it was determined that if it was not documented that the inmate did anything wrong then it never happened and the supervisor was reaching for ways to exonerate himself.

In summary, the medical record corroborated the fact that the inmate sustained injuries on the date and approximate time that he reported to medical personnel an unprovoked attack on his person by a correctional supervisor. If there is no inmate report of infraction (rule violation report) or no incident report this means that the inmate did not violate any inmate rules of discipline or any criminal statutes; therefore, why was physical force used against him. Remember, if all the facts and circumstances are not documented in writing by staff, it never occurred as later reported by staff only after being served with a lawsuit so the correctional agency and staff are liable pursuant to the 14th Amendment to the US. Constitution and the inmate's remedy will be 42 United States Code, Section 1983, which could be a financial remedy for the inmate in addition to reasonable attorney fees entitled under United States Code. Sawyer v. Asbury (2012) and numerous other cases following the same court ruling have decided that provocation by mere insults or threatening language does not justify a use of physical force by correctional staff. Indeed, mere words without more do not constitute provocation or aggression by the inmate speaking those words.

From the case in point above, you can see the importance of documenting all incidents and serious allegations. If the facility does not document and investigate all incidents they make themselves liable for civil law suits. In addition, it shows the court that the correctional agency failed to follow their own rules and regulations of documenting and reporting.

If the agency does not clean its own house (discipline staff as appropriate) report and investigate incidents, and prevent same from occurring again, state and federal courts will have the agency reporting and sending copies of all future incidents to court appointed agencies such as state and local boards of correction for scrutiny or in some extreme cases scrutiny by special agents of the Federal Bureau of Investigations. It is the investigating officer's job to show who acted properly and who failed to follow policies, procedures, agency work rules, state law and inmate rules of discipline.

If your investigation shows that staff are in violation of policy, some type of progressive disciplinary action must be taken and documented so that the agency does not create an atmosphere that condones violations of policy and inmate rights. This goes a long way in mitigating legal judgments against correctional agencies. It also shows staff that violations of rules will not be tolerated. If staff see that violations occur and management overlooks them, the facility will see a drastic increase in staff violations of all types.

U.S. District Court - Deficiencies in Facility Internal Investigations

Lyons (1989) reports on <u>Charles Fisher, et. al. v. Richard Koehler, et al.</u> (1987), the court noted the following deficiencies after three national experts reviewed numerous internal investigation reports from one correctional facility. The three experts all reported that if the investigators had submitted the reports to them they would have returned every single one for significant deficiencies. Upon a review of contemporary literature on correctional internal investigations available evidence suggest that these same deficiencies still exist in year 2015 in correctional facilities across the country and this is the major reason that I wrote this book to remedy the situation. :

- **Not progressing along logical lines:** The accumulation and presentation of evidence does not illustrate a sequential, orderly and logical thought progression therefore, conclusions do not follow from the evidence presented.
- **Contradictions Not Pursued**: Oftentimes there are contradictions in witnesses' statements that must be pursued by the investigator. One cannot simply disregard contradictions in custodial staff statements but address them in inmate statements not only should the investigator

include all contradictions but they must also pursue and resolve contradictions if possible.

- **Treatment of Medical Evidence:** The court also stated that medical evidence is used primarily to discredit inmates' statements and to uphold the staff version. The absence of a visible injury to correspond to a blow an inmate says he received is taken as evidence that the inmate is not truthful; the same scrutiny is not given to officers' injuries or lack thereof. Where medical findings do support the inmate's account, they are weighed less heavily. In many cases, where inmates have been injured consistent with their accounts, it is arbitrarily asserted by the lay internal investigators that the inmates' injuries are not serious enough to support their testimony.

To assist investigators in reading and analyzing medical reports the "SOAP" format is submitted below:

S - Subjective - what the inmate/patient reports to medical personnel, claims or says the problem is.

O - Objective - what the medical staff actually observes

A - Assessment - the medical staff's diagnosis of any injuries found

P - Plan - what the medical staff plans to do to treat the inmate/patient

The investigator should look for the "soap" format (information) when evaluating medical evidence. If the medical report does not contain the above information you should request it from medical personnel. If you cannot read the doctor's writing you should ask the doctor or nurse to explain the report so it can be more easily understood.

Medical evidence can mean the difference between a guilt or innocence determination by a state or federal court against a correctional agency. Case in Point: An officer reported that he used physical force in self defense by using arm and body holds to restrain an assaultive inmate who refused to lock in his cell for count. The officer further reported that he and the inmate fell to the floor and the officer handcuffed the inmate and notified his supervisor.

The inmate reported that he and the officer had a previous disagreement and the officer told him to just wait until count time. When it was time for the afternoon lockdown (count), the officer opened all the cells but his and locked all of the other inmates in their cells. The officer then approached him, cursed him and dared him to fight. When the inmate refused to fight and stated that he would report the incident to supervisors, the officer began punching him with clenched fist knocking him to the floor and stomping him in his side while he was on the floor.

Medical Evidence: The inmate medical report in brief showed:

Subjective: The inmate reported to the doctor that he was not allowed to lock in his cell along with other inmates. He was assaulted by the officer with clenched fist for no reason and when he fell to the floor the officer stomped him repeatedly on the left side of his body and in his rib area.

Objective: The doctor reported that he observed multiple bruises and contusions on both sides of the inmate's face, redness, a split lower lip with dried blood and redness on the left side of his ribs that appeared in the shape of a large shoe print.

Assessment: The inmate was determined to have soreness to the touch on his left rib cage, minor cuts, bruises, scrapes to both arms, a spit lower lip, bruises and contusions on both sides of his face along with swelling to the right side of his face.

Plan: The various wounds were cleaned, an ice pack was used to decrease swelling to the right side of face, and the inmate was given Motrin for pain. The inmate was transferred to the local hospital for X-rays of his ribs and a note was made to return the inmate to the facility medical clinic for follow-up evaluation on the following day.

You are the investigator of this incident, who is obviously telling the truth and who is lying? The officer said that he used "arm and body holds to restrain the inmate" as they fell to the floor. The inmate said that he was punched, knocked to the floor and stomped in his side.

The doctor does not know the inmate and does not know the officer. The doctor's medical report is consistent with the inmate's testimony. The medical evidence is inconsistent with the officer's report of physical force used against the inmate. The investigator must pursue this major contradiction between the inmate's version and the officer's version and resolve the contradiction. Remember the court said that in many cases, where inmates have been injured consistent with their accounts, it is arbitrarily asserted by the internal investigators that the inmates' injures are not serious enough to support their testimony.

In the above case the findings of the investigator's report read that the inmate only had minor injury to his ribs that occurred when he fell and the incident occurred as reported by the officer. An investigator cannot have findings and conclusions contrary to medical evidence without a strong justification.

Failure to Pursue Fundamental Questions: The court said that fundamental questions are often not answered and sometimes are not even addressed. These include factual questions such as how much force was actually used and who initiated a physical altercation and questions of compliance with policy such as whether there were any alternatives to a use of physical force or whether less force could have been used. These questions are sometimes obscured with "boilerplate recitations" such as the force was "minimal and necessary" or "within the department's guidelines". In some cases, lines of inquiry that raise issues of staff misconduct are simply dropped, in other cases, the investigator calls for further investigation by someone else that either does not occur or is done in a biased and superficial manner.

Investigators should avoid general terminology that does not actually describe what happened. For example, "minimal force was used", or "the inmate approached in a threatening manner". Investigators should discipline themselves to avoid accepting "catch-all" phrases. When a participant tells the investigator that the aggressor approached in a threatening manner, it is incumbent upon the investigator not to let the statement end there, but to ask additional questions to allow the individual to expound on such a phrase. Would a correctional employee with similar training and experience perceive the inmate's actions to be in a threatening manner? Would a fair and reasonable person sitting on a civil court jury perceive the inmate's actions to be "in a threatening manner"? The question for further probing is what constitutes a threatening manner?

Procedures With Respect to Inmate Witnesses: Often little or no effort is made to identify and interview inmate witnesses, even when they could be readily identified. When an area is "canvassed" for witnesses with little or no response, or when apparent witnesses are reluctant to comment, investigators do not make any subsequent effort to conduct witness interviews in a private setting away from sight and hearing of staff and other inmates.

Evaluation of Witness' Statements: A double standard is applied to inmate and staff statements. When inmate witness statements contain apparent inconsistencies or omissions, the statements are generally discounted without further inquiry, while omissions and inconsistencies in staff's statements are ignored. Indeed, omissions and inconsistencies in inmate statements are magnified and sometimes manufactured. The court stated that an inmate's statement is just as credible as an officer's statement; therefore, they are equally weighed on a scale until there is some credible evidence to tip the scale in either the inmate or the officer's side.

Lack of Impartiality: One cannot investigate an incident in which one was involved in. If one was involved as an eye witness or participant then that person should not be the investigating officer. It shows a lack of impartiality and objectivity.

Resort to Speculation and Assumption to Exonerate Staff: Fictional or speculative rationales and assumptions unsupported in the investigative report are employed to justify staff conduct or discredit inmate statements that conflict with the staff version of events.

Case in Point: The court provided the following example: An inmate sustained a minor lip abrasion and a contusion of his face, the inmate said that he was punched in the face by a correctional officer and identified him. Upon investigation, the officer denied the inmate's allegation and stated that he had no knowledge of the incident. The investigating officer's findings and conclusions stated that the inmate may have self-inflicted "these minor injuries to lessen the impact of an anticipated disciplinary report". There is nothing in the investigative record to support the claim that the inmate self-inflicted his injuries or any reason why he anticipated a disciplinary report from the officer.

References:

Fisher et al. v. Koehler et al., U.S. District Court, Southern District of New York, 83 Civ., 2128, (MEL), June (1987).

Lyons, D. P. (1989). Facility investigations training manual. Richard Koehler, Commissioner, Unpublished Manuscript, City of New York, Department of Correction

Sawyer v. Asbury, 861 F. Supp. 2d 737 (S.D.W. Va. 2012)

Chapter 4

DEFINITIONS AND TYPES OF EVIDENCE

Chapter Learning Objectives

- Define evidence
- List the categories of evidence
- Identify signs of altering documentary evidence
- Collect, identify and mark evidence
- List the steps involved in creating a chain of custody
- Evaluate oral and written statements
- Differentiate between fact, hearsay, opinion and conclusion

Evidence

According to Gifis (1984), evidence is "all the means by which any alleged matter of fact, the truth of which is submitted to investigation. . . is either established or disproved" (p. 185). In all types of detention center or prison investigations the investigator must refer to the evidence that supports his/her findings and conclusions. As reiterated by Hess and Orthmann (2010a) and Lyons (1989), the primary purpose of conducting an investigation is: identify, locate and preserve evidence. "It is the process of discovering, collecting, preparing, identifying and presenting evidence to determine what happened and who is responsible" (p. 6). "An allegation is not itself evidence but rather is something to be proved or disproved through the introduction of competent administrative evidence" (Gifis, 1984, p. 165). The rules of evidence that apply to a correctional facility are less stringent than with police on the street. Conducting an administrative investigation inside a correctional institution usually involves testimonial evidence, documentary evidence, demonstrative or physical evidence. Klein (1980) defines evidence as the means by which any alleged matter of fact under investigation is either established or disproved.

Categories of Evidence

As previously stated above, generally evidence is categorized as one of four types, that is, testimonial, documentary, demonstrative and/or physical (Hess & Orthmann, 2010b, p. 122-123).

Testimonial Evidence: This includes eyewitness evidence, the statements obtained through interviews and interrogations of what was seen and heard. The statements given by witnesses must be observed facts and not personal opinions or conclusions.

Documentary Evidence: consists of writings, audio and video recordings, reports, letters, logbooks forms, files and so on. This includes information which is gained from documents such as log books, officer and inmate written reports, photographs, sketches, and so on. Pictures, diagrams, maps or similar items is also referred to as demonstrative evidence.

Physical Evidence: is anything that is tangible that helps to establish the facts of an incident. It is something that can be physically seen, smelled or touched, it can also be a liquid. Some police agencies often refer to physical evidence as "real evidence" or "hard evidence". A common classification of physical evidence is direct and indirect evidence. "Direct evidence establishes proof of a fact without any other evidence. Indirect evidence merely tends to incriminate a person--for instance a suspect's footprints found near the crime scene. Indirect evidence is also called circumstantial evidence" (Hess & Orthmann, 2010, p. 123).

Corroborating Evidence: any evidence supplementary to that already given or listed and tending to strengthen or confirm it. "It is additional evidence of a different character on the same point" (Gifis, 1984, p. 103).

Hearsay: The Federal Rules of Evidence defines hearsay as: "A statement other than one made by the declarant while testifying in court offered in evidence to prove the truth of the matter asserted" (Section 801). For our purpose, it is evidence written or oral, that is not based on the personal knowledge or eyewitness account of the witness. Oftentimes, it is based on what someone else had said or what they have allegedly witnessed.

When writing the report of investigation, investigators should refer to the evidence that forms the basis for their findings and conclusions.

Chain of Custody

Our focus here is on physical evidence or tangible objects such as homemade weapons (shanks/shivs), narcotics or other physical contraband, namely evidence other than testimonial that the investigator must safeguard for disciplinary hearings or criminal prosecution. Hess and Hess (2010), define integrity of evidence as the requirement that any item introduced in court has to be one and the same condition as when it was recovered at the crime scene. This is documented by what is referred to as chain of custody. Modern evidence bags used in correctional facilities contain a chain of custody printed right on the plastic see-through bag. Each and every individual taking possession of evidence should be listed on the bag. For example, Officer Smith recovered a shank hidden on the person of inmate John Doe during a search. Upon surrendering the weapon to the investigating officer, the investigator list the name and identifying information on the officer who recovered the weapon and the name of the investigating officer who received the evidence. If Internal Affairs receives the weapon from the investigating officer, the investigator will write his name on the evidence bag and the last person in receipt of the evidence. If the case goes to court, the chain of custody must show that this is in fact the same weapon recovered on the scene and these are all of the individuals who had possession of the weapon at any time.

The officer who recovered the weapon should also etch his initials on the weapon and the date. This will show the court or a disciplinary board that this is in fact the same weapon recovered on the scene on a particular date and time. Prior to placing the weapon in the evidence bag the officer should lay it out on the glass of the photocopy machine, lay a ruler beside the weapon and make several copies. The photo copies will go forward with the report of investigation as the weapon should be safeguarded in the Chief of Security's safe. Anyone reading the report will be able to see the weapon and the actual length of it. The weapon should not be handled so as to smudge or destroy fingerprints especially in a case for possible prosecution. If possible, handle the weapon with latex gloves safely with the finger tips to safeguard any DNA or fingerprints. If placed in a loosely fitting paper bag the prints should not smudge. The plastic evidence bag may very well smudge the prints where they are unrecognizable from the moisture that forms inside the bag. A physical evidence and/or contraband log should be maintained in the safe so that any item removed from the safe will be properly documented as to the name, date, time and reason the evidence/contraband was removed and/or disposition of the evidence/contraband or return.

Evaluation of Oral and Written Statements

Once the investigator has completed collecting evidence it should be evaluated. Since direct evidence establishes proof of a fact without any other evidence it is the most important piece of evidence to explain what happened and who did it. Direct evidence usually consists of the testimony of eyewitnesses, that is, evidence that tends to establish a fact at issue. For example, an officer's statement that he saw an inmate steal another inmate's property is direct evidence that the accused inmate committed the theft. When evaluating evidence you should ask yourself the following questions. Are the witnesses versions of the event similar? If not, are the differences substantial? For example, two witnesses describe an altercation between two inmates Brown and Smith. The first witness reports that it occurred at 1 P.M., the second witness reports that it occurred at 1:15 P.M. This discrepancy in their statements would not be substantial with respect to whether such an altercation took place. However, if the two witnesses disagree as to which one of the two inmates was the aggressor and threw the first punch, the investigator is left with a substantial discrepancy to resolve.

Are the participant's versions of the event consistent with the medical evidence? If not, is there a valid reason for the participants to erroneously describe the injury? For example, an officer reports that he only used body holds to break up a minor fight between two inmates; however, the medical evaluation indicates that the inmate has a laceration to his forehead and other injuries inconsistent with the officer's testimony. This discrepancy may indicate that the officer did not wish to give the full details of the unusual occurrence. On the other hand, the inmate may have been injured by the other inmate during the altercation. The investigator must address this inconsistency. The investigator must rely on medical evidence fairly, not just to discredit inmates' statements and uphold staff versions. Investigators should also realize that inmates may overstate the seriousness of an injury in order to gain attention to their report of incident. Thus, the medical evidence may not fully support the inmate's claim. For example, an inmate may claim that he was beaten about his head but no injury is detected in the medical report. This does not necessarily mean that the inmate's account is completely false--the inmate may, in fact, have been hit in the head several times and there is no visible injury but there should be an explanation in the investigator's report regarding the inmate's allegation and the inconsistency with medical evidence.

Similarly, if an officer reports that he was assaulted, to wit, punched in the face by an inmate that resulted in the officer using physical force pursuant to policy, the investigator should determine whether the officer's injuries, if any, are consistent with the account of the incident and documented medical evidence. That is, an officer's injury must be evaluated and investigated with the same degree of scrutiny as inmate injury reports. Pursuing an objective quest for truth, the investigator must weigh the medical evidence along with all other evidence to reach a conclusion as to what actually occurred.

If witnesses' versions are similar, is there reason to believe that the witnesses' versions were the result of collaboration? This may depend upon how expediently the witnesses were separated and not allowed to agree with one another to the same story. The similarity may not reflect the truth, and may be an attempt by those involved to make up a story. The speed with which you begin to investigate the unusual occurrence will be an important factor in determining whether interviews were conducted before collaboration could occur. There must be a valid reason to believe that statements were the result of collaboration and that they are untruthful. Similarity may mean that the witnesses all saw the same thing very clearly. Also, not all collaborative statements are false. If you have reason to believe that witnesses came together to concoct a story, you should be able to test the idea by interviewing the witnesses separately. It may also be helpful for the investigator to reenact the scene to verify if it was possible for the incident to have occurred as reported by inmates or staff.

It is unacceptable for an inmate to write a statement about an incident and have all of the other inmates sign the same statement as alleged eyewitnesses. In such cases, the signers should be interviewed separately out of sight and hearing of all of the other inmates, informed that you will not discuss their statements or written testimony with any other inmates, then interview the inmate and request a written report of his testimony. If the inmate reports that he has difficulty writing, it is permissible for another inmate that he trusts to write the statement for him and have the inmate sign the report as the writer while the inmate witness makes his mark of signature on the report. I prefer that if the inmate permits, the investigator can write the inmate's statement, have the inmate place his mark on the report and have an impartial staff member preferably a counselor, religious leader, or teacher (non-security employee) sign the report as a witness that the inmate requested the investigator to write his report and it has been written free from duress and undue influence.

If there are substantial differences, can the inconsistencies be accounted for in terms of witnesses' location relative to the incident? Witnesses may have different perceptions depending on their proximity and angle of view, and in many cases, some witnesses will see only the beginning or middle of an incident and others may see only the end. If an alleged eyewitness reports that he in fact saw the entire incident, the investigator should question the alleged eyewitness as to the exact location he was in when the incident occurred, the lighting, did he have an unobstructed view, if he wears glasses, did he have his glasses on, is he color blind and a variety of other probing questions.

Case in Point: I investigated an inmate allegation of an unprovoked assault and battery upon his person by another inmate. One of the alleged inmate eyewitness reports stated that as he exited his cell, "I saw the whole thing" and wrote a statement in support of the alleged inmate assailant. I went to the housing unit, and stood at the exact same location as the alleged inmate eyewitness. I discovered that the maintenance department had not yet followed up on an officer's work order to replace burned out lighting in the housing unit. And it was impossible for the alleged eyewitness to have seen anything at all based upon distance, poor lighting and inmate obstructions namely, the crowd gathered around the assault.

Conflicting statements should be evaluated not only in terms of evaluating medical evidence but also in terms of the relationship of the alleged eyewitness making the statement to inmate participants involved in the incident. Is the witness hostile (adverse)? An adverse witness is one whose relationship to the opposing party may be such that the testimony could be prejudiced against that person and untruthful. For example, an inmate housed in administrative segregation reclassified as a management problem because he is assaultive to staff and has continuous disciplinary reports for disrespecting staff and not following facility rules. This type of inmate may be biased in his testimony against the staff. On the other hand inmates who are classified according to the violence perpetrated in the facility or troublesome inmates may be the ones most likely to evoke untruthful testimony by staff, that is, staff may be biased against such inmates. If a witness actually displays such physical behavior and hostility, your report should describe the activity in terms of the inmate's possible credibility.

Are any of the principle participants in an incident close friends of any witness or witnesses? The existence of a close relationship between a perpetrator and alleged witnesses may lead the witnesses to falsify their statements in favor of the one to whom a close relationship exists. If witness bias can be established then the witnesses' credibility is questionable. Naturally, close friends, relatives and codefendants could have credibility issues that should be stated. One would be very surprised if a close friend, relative or codefendant did not back-up the statements of the perpetrator whether truthful or untruthful. Does any witness stand to gain or lose anything of value as a consequence of his testimony? For example, will the inmate or staff member avoid disciplinary action by relating the incident favorable to themselves. Each of these questions suggests a motive for any of the witnesses to be untruthful.

Is there available any documentary or testimonial evidence that the witness has previously made statements or written reports that are inconsistent with his/her present testimony or report? If so, the present testimony or report raises a reasonable doubt as to the veracity of any of his/her statements. In some cases oral or spontaneous statements made when the person's memory was more recent or at the time of the incident are generally more accurate than later statements.

It must be mentioned that minor inconsistencies should not be used to discredit one's version of an incident. Similarly, the failure of a witness to mention a detail in the incident does not automatically discredit the testimony of the witness. Instead, it should be the basis for additional probing in cases of a conflict of evidence, the truth should be sought by presentation of evidence and by weighing the credibility of the respective witnesses, not by the mere number of statements on one side or the other.

Investigators should not automatically assume that either staff or inmate reports are truthful. Bennett and Hess (2001), state that a person who may resort to not being fully truthful or being untruthful usually ends up on the defensive and may become entangled in a web of deceit. And, that it is difficult to repeat lies consistently in that each lie sounds better than the last one; therefore, the story becomes more distorted with mistakes and exaggerations. Compare the reports of factual information received (corroborated by some evidence) and assess against the other reports received.

To assess the credibility of witnesses the Council of Canadian Administrative Tribunals (2000), suggest that investigators pursue the following questions but not necessarily in the order presented below:

- Does the witness' statement conflict with direct evidence or seem improbable?
- Are there any documented contradictions in the report?
- Is there information and belief that the report is biased?
- Does the report provide misleading information?
- Are there contradictions in the witness' report?
- Does the witness report amount to hearsay information?
- What is the basis of the witness' knowledge, is it second-hand information based on something the witness heard?
- Has the witness made statements in the past that is inconsistent with what he is now reporting?
- Was the witness in a position to effectively perceive the facts as he reported it?
- Does the witness have any motives or personal interest that affect the outcome?

Wise and Safer (2007), reminds investigators to beware of eyewitness error. I can surely attest to that statement. As a New York City Police Officer assigned to patrol duties, I was asked to participate in a police line-up due to the fact that they were one person short of the number needed for a lineup to identify an armed robbery suspect captured shortly thereafter with a firearm. I immediately changed out of the regular police uniform and put on civilian clothing. One alleged eyewitness to the robbery picked me out of the line-up as a positive identification of the perpetrator. She was shocked to find out from the patrol supervisor that not only did they capture the perpetrator leaving the scene who looked nothing like this writer but also that on the date and time of the armed robbery, I was routinely assigned to the police station for eight hours of administrative duties. Indeed, Huff (1987) reports that eyewitness error is the leading cause of wrongful criminal convictions. Eyewitness statements must be corroborated by some other evidence.

Drawing Conclusions and Evaluating Evidence

Investigators must be aware of the differences between what is considered fact, hearsay, opinion and conclusion.

Fact: "A fact is an event that has occurred or circumstances that exist, events whose actual occurrence or existence is to be determined by the evidence" (Gifis, 1984, p.175). Something that is true or actually happened.

Hearsay: "Unverified information received from another," it is oral or written testimony based on the reports of others rather than on the personal knowledge of a witness (Webster's II, New College Dictionary, 2005, p. 523). For example, it may be reported to the investigator that inmate John Doe was born in Brooklyn, New York, on July 04, 1990. The investigator has no other information about the birth of Doe, just his statement. The investigator was not present on the date that Doe was born nor does he have his birth record or driver's license; therefore, an accurate report is, inmate John Doe orally reported to this investigator during an oral interview on date, time and location, that he was born on July 04, 1990, in Brooklyn, New York. The *fact* is that Doe made a statement to the investigator about his birth date and birth place. As far as the investigator is concerned the content of the statement is *hearsay* until such time that is verified as a fact.

Opinion: "A belief or idea held with confidence but not substantiated by direct proof or knowledge" (Webster's II, New College Dictionary, 2005, p. 787). According to Dienstein (1975), an opinion is a personal estimation approximating a judgment, but falls short of the certainty of conviction usually attributed to a judgment. It is an idea or impression or a notion resulting from a personal sentiment. Opinions of the investigator are usually not part of the investigative report unless it is the policy of the department to permit the expression of opinion in specifically designated parts of the report. Where policy permits reports to provide for an expression of opinion, it is usually limited to the investigator's estimation of the credibility of the various witnesses and/or informants. The investigative report should specifically state: *"It is the opinion of this investigator"* based upon the following evidence that. . . ." Dienstein (1975), reminds investigators that an opinion is an opinion because there is insufficient evidence to support it and that is why opinions are usually not permitted in the investigative report. This does not imply that the investigator should not formulate opinions during the course of the investigation. His/her opinions may serve as guides for further action when he seems to reach a dead end.

Conclusion: A decision reached after objective analysis of facts, circumstances, evidence and possible inductive and/or deductive reasoning. A conclusion involves the drawing of an inference, what is, or appears to be necessary and logical consequences of preceding propositions, information, or evidence (Dienstein, 1975). For example, arriving at the scene of an assault on an inmate with a weapon involved (stabbing), the officer finds the body of an inmate laying on the floor and one other inmate with a shank in his hand standing over the body. The preceding statement may be put in the following manner:

1. There is an apparent assault with a weapon in the housing unit.
2. The inmate has a homemade weapon (shank) in his hand and is standing over the body.
3. The inmate with the shank committed an assault and battery with a weapon. This preceding sentence is a conclusion derived from inductive reasoning. Simply stated, inductive reasoning says if you are presented with "A', and then "B" the logical conclusion is "C".

The above example is also presented to make the point that it is possible to draw faulty conclusions from facts. On the other hand, it is possible to draw valid conclusions from inductive reasoning. A conclusion does not become a fact until verification is made through further information and evidence.

In summary, Dienstein (1975), states that a fact proves itself whereas a conclusion requires corroborating evidence, that is, evidence supplementary to that already established and tending to strengthen or confirm the evidence. A conclusion is reasoned whereas a fact is a reality. The investigator must be able to separate fact, hearsay, opinion and conclusion in the report of investigation.

When evaluating documentary evidence such as housing unit log books make sure you confiscate the log books immediately before evidence is lost, destroyed or altered. Be alert for signs of tampering in sequentially numbered page log books or forms (suicide watch and other forms) as listed below:

- Different handwriting
- Obvious changes in original entries
- Existence of discrepancies
- Use of white-out and crossing out of information (rather than drawing a straight line through the entry and initialing it)
- Simultaneous entries (when it appears that several hours worth of entries in a logbook or form were all made at the

same time instead of entries being made every 30 minutes or every hour at irregular intervals)
- Liquids such as water or coffee spilled on page(s) in order to cause the ink to run and render the page(s) not readable.
- Erasure marks
- Squeezing in entries
- Missing pages

If you need to make notations about the written record do not write on the original. Your markings may cause confusion as to what was originally in the record.

Photographing of Evidence

As previously stated all evidence should be photographed either with a camera, video recorder or photocopy machine. Evidence such as weapons, blood, and controlled substances should be photographed in the location where found if at all possible prior to handling. In cases of the employer's workers compensation investigations photograph elements of the weather that may have caused an employee's injury that is visible on the floor, a broken chair in the location that it came apart and caused alleged injury, something that fell from the ceiling and so on. Photographs should be taken from eye level, that is the height that most people view things. Remember the age old saying that: *"a picture is worth a thousand words"*. Through photography, the investigator will be able to reproduce evidence in its original state.

Once again, do not allow anything to be moved prior to photographing. If staff or inmates have moved something prior to photographing, document the scene as you found it. If the investigator should attempt to relocate the evidence where witnesses state that it was originally, if the case goes to court it could be stated that the investigator staged the scene or you altered the evidence.

Photographs should be taken from general to specific, that is, a long-range view of the area, victim, notes or letters and any weapons. Specific photographs should show close-up photos of victims and any evidence found. During specific photographing the investigator should concentrate on wounds of the victim, weapon, physical plant intact, damaged (escape), blood patterns, and so on. Photographs should be taken from various angles to allow for viewing all parts of the room. This will allow for no hidden areas in the room and no obstructions to the viewer of the photograph. Victims should be photographed from various angles.

No contemporary correctional institution should be without a video recorder although in some small rural detention facilities one may not find a video recorder for documenting riots and major disturbances and to show that facility emergency response personnel followed policy and the prevailing state law by making every effort to gain compliance with lawful orders and to document unlawful actions of inmates. Video records may also be used almost anytime that there is an anticipated use of physical force from this writer's experience, when inmates see that you are videotaping the incident, they will cease and desist any unlawful actions and there may not be a need for physical force. Video taping is the highly recommended method of documenting evidence for court presentation. As is required of most correctional emergency response team training, the video operator should verbally identify himself/herself on the video, state the date and time of the incident, the institution and the unusual occurrence being taped. The video tape should be labeled with the date, time and location of the unusual occurrence, the facility name, and the inmate's name. The video should be placed in a secure library for future use such as presentation at court.

In this writer's experience, it is best to have two video recorders taping at the same time in riots and major disturbances. One recorder focused on medium and close-up specific activities as they occur and one camera on a tripod with a long range shot of the entire overall scene. Always ensure that there are extra fresh batteries on hand for each camera. We will discuss riots and major disturbances in more detail in Chapter 6. The investigator will also find it useful to use sketches to supplement photographs so that the viewer can see the relationships of objects to one another, the surrounding area and to show whether or not alleged witnesses' statements are accurate. The sketch of locality also assist the investigator in showing the physical location, walls, hallways, entrances, exits, inmate movement, designs of housing areas and so forth. A sketch of details describes the specific scene of the incident, for example, a prison cell and its contents within a housing unit. Using a ruler, compass and other tools anyone can draw a sketch. Since I can not draw well, I used "stickmen" (as young children draw) to depict staff or inmates.

A sketch will also provide the reviewer of your report with details of the location that a photograph cannot and it may be useful when interviewing witnesses. It is important to note on your sketch that it is not drawn to scale. In case you are summoned to court to testify, you do not want to damage a prosecution's case regarding the exact footage of an area. Instead of estimating footage, use a tape measure or a rolling distance measurer that will provide the investigator with the exact distances. With so many new prisons and detention centers being built today, there may be some 8 1/2 x 11 or 8 1/2 x 14 architectural drawings of various locations within the facility to assist the investigator.

References

Bennett, W.W. and Hess, K.M. (2004). Criminal investigation. (7th ed.). California: Wadsworth/Thompson Learning

Council of Canadian Administrative Tribunals, June 11-13, 2000. Assessing credibility of witness: a practical guide Annual Conference

Dienstein, W. (1975). How to write a narrative investigation report. Springfield, IL: Charles O. Thomas

Federal Rules of Evidence, Section 803 Hearsay Rule Defined. United States Courts and Magistrates, 1982.

Gifis, S. H. (1984). <u>Law dictionary</u>, (2nd ed.) New York: Barron's Education Series

Hess, K.M. and Orthmann (2010a). <u>Criminal investigation</u>. (9th ed.) N.Y.: Delmar Cengage Learning

Hess, K.M. and Orthmann (2010b). <u>Criminal investigation</u>. (9th ed.) Clinton Park,N.Y.: Delmar Cengage Learning, pages 122-123

Huff, R.C. (1987). <u>Wrongful conviction: societal tolerance of injustice</u>. 4 Res: In Soc. Prob. & Pub Pol'y 99, 103

Klein, I. (1980). <u>Law of evidence for police</u>, (2nd ed.) Minn.: West Publishing Co.

Lyons, D. & Foreman, M. (1989), City of New York, Dept. of Correction, <u>facility investigations training manual</u>. Richard Koehler, Commissioner. Unpublished Manuscript approved for N.Y.C. Dept. of Correction

Wise, R.A. & Safer, Martin, A. (2009). <u>A method for analyzing the accuracy of eyewitness testimony in criminal cases</u>. Court Review - Volume 48

<u>Webster's II New College Dictionary</u>. (2005), (3rd ed.). Boston, New York: Houghton Mifflin Co.

Chapter 5

NARRATIVE INVESTIGATION REPORT

Chapter Learning Objectives:

- Define report of investigation
- Explain the basic considerations of remaining objective
- Define active versus passive writing
- Explain correct paragraph structure and format
- Write a narrative report of investigation using one of the models provided

---

In detention centers and prisons a supervisor cannot begin conducting a preliminary investigation until all emergency conditions have been satisfied, the scene has been properly secured, order restored, medical services provided to all participants, victims and witnesses. Prior to beginning the report of investigation some investigators obtain a one-quarter inch or larger three-ring binder depending upon the anticipated amount of data expected to be collected, a three-hole punch and dividers depending upon the seriousness of the incident. This allows for good organization, manageability of numerous statements received and attachments. The accumulated data regarding the serious incident are placed in the binder in chronological order with their attachments and possible photographs, sketches and other evidentiary documentation. Concise headings and sub-headings centered at the beginning of the page for short reports (three to eight pages--no need for a binder) or dividers for lengthy reports (eight or more pages). Headings or dividers may include such information as: first response and action taken, preservation of the scene, evidence collected, witnesses statements and so on.

Structuring the Narrative Report

A word of caution about structuring the narrative report. The reader of your report should not have to read several pages or the entire report before finding out what really happened. This can be very annoying and time consuming for a facility administrator who may have a lot of reports to review. I begin a report of investigation by stating the: who, what, when, where, how, why, and what action taken in the topic (first) sentence; therefore reviewers of the report will know from the first paragraph what this report is all about. Busy administrators do not want to read long drawn out reports that rehash insignificant points over and over again without getting to the crux of the incident. Although concise, reports should not sacrifice clarity or completeness.

Based upon this writer's experience it is best to limit paragraphs to approximately 125 words or less discussing one subject in each paragraph. The report should be written in the past tense, that is, depict events that have already occurred.

The final report should consist of a complete synthesis of the information that you gathered. Although you can exercise some discretion regarding the information you included in the final report, you have an ethical obligation to address legitimate concerns that surfaced during the course of the investigation.

After writing the topic sentence, you can begin by stating what you were told by staff, inmate victims, inmate witnesses and facility visitors. I recommend that you use a separate paragraph for each person that you interview that has a different statement as to what happened. Briefly summarize that person's verbal testimony and compare their initial statements with their written report that you will ask them to submit thus putting their statements in writing. Oftentimes you will find that there are significant differences in statements after the victim, witness, participant or suspect has had a chance to talk to others and/or manufacture statements. If you find major inconsistencies in the verbal and written statements you have an obligation to state the inconsistency in your report and try to resolve it. After summarizing the information that is pertinent to the incident from all reports received, include the original report chronologically listed and addressed as an attachment at the end of the report.

The final report should also state the actions taken by the investigator to gather evidence and follow investigative protocol as follows:

- Did you ensure immediate medical care for victim, witnesses or perpetrator?
- Did you observe any physical evidence such as blood on suspects shoes, clothing, cuts, scrapes and/or bruises on participant's knuckles that may refute their oral testimony of not being involved in the incident?
- Did you authorize a search of the housing unit or cell for discarded clothing containing blood or for weapons?
- If weapons were used and confiscated, did you ensure the weapon was photographed and/or photocopied with a ruler beside it as corroborating evidence?
- Did you ensure that a chain of custody was initiated for evidence for possible criminal prosecution or disciplinary action, and did you secure such evidence, and where?
- Did you canvass the area for witnesses and ensure that the witnesses and participants were separated from one another to ensure objective statements were submitted.
- Did you record spontaneous utterances made during the investigation or initial response on the scene and later compare those utterances with written statements submitted?
- If inmate witnesses refused to make statements or submit written reports did you document this refusal and/or contact

them at a later time to see if they would make a statement. Also did you identify the possible witnesses in case law enforcement or internal affairs wishes to interview them?

- Did you assign additional staff from other areas of the facility so that the staff participants or witnesses could seek medical treatment and write their reports?
- Did you review or assign someone else to review recorded activity on facility 24 hour security cameras so that you can view the actions of all concerned in the incident?
- If required, did you make notification according to established policy and procedure?
- Did you ensure that disciplinary action was written on inmate participants?

The concluding paragraph should state the evidence relied upon to corroborate the investigator's findings, conclusions and possible recommendations. The evidence relied upon could consist of physical evidence confiscated from the scene, medical evidence, visual evidence, review of recorded security cameras, staff reports, visitor's statements, inmate witness reports and so on. Your report should explain the steps that you followed to gather evidence and analyze findings based on that evidence. The investigator must show that the findings, conclusions and recommendations are based on the evidence submitted with the report.

Report Format Number One

The format of the closing report should consist of four items: (1.) the introduction, (2.) the body of the report, (3.) findings and conclusions and, (4.) recommendations. This report should be written on agency letterhead in the form of: To, From, Date, and Subject. Some agencies may have a specific format preprinted on forms. Or, agencies may use color-coded pre-printed forms.

1. Introduction: A basic explanation of what took place. It identifies the unusual incident and should also relate any allegation, who made the allegation, the date and time of the

incident and a brief summary of the incident. As previously stated, the topic sentence is where the investigator briefly records the: who, what, when, where, how, why of the incident and what actions, if any, taken by the investigator? Sample introductory sentence of inmate injury report of investigation: Submitted herein is a report of investigation on the alleged injury reported by inmate John Doe, #000-00-000, on March 04, 2015, on or about 1615 hours, as the inmate exited the dining hall. There were no staff or inmate witnesses to this alleged incident although there were two supervisors standing at the exit/entrance door and five officers lining both sides of the hallway outside the dining hall and numerous inmates from Pod A, exiting the cafeteria the same time the incident allegedly occurred. Inmate Doe reported that that as he exited the dining hall, he slipped on the wet floor and fell backward injuring his back. This investigator had the inmate transported to the medical clinic under the supervision of chief nurse Jane Doe. Medical found no injuries to the inmate including an evaluation of X-rays. NOTE: In this topic sentence it is stated: When? Who? Where? What? How? Why? And what actions taken by the investigator?

2. Body: The body of the report is a narrative of the activities performed. It is an impartial and objective presentation of the facts established through the investigative process. It makes reference to the evidence that support the facts and findings. The body of the report should also include all work done to bring the investigation to a close. This includes witness reports submitted as attachments, other document collection, staff reports and so on submitted as attachments. The body of the report also includes information learned by the investigator upon viewing facility video recording (copy submitted as an attachment). This information should be logically organized and presented in a chronologically, concise and orderly manner so that reviewers will be able to follow your line of thought. You must also remember that your report may be reviewed by attorneys, law enforcement personnel and/or criminal/

civil court personnel; therefore, do not use detention or jail slang in the report because outside personnel will not understand what you are talking about.

Findings and Conclusions: In this part of the report the investigator relates the outcome or result of the investigative process using factual determinations based upon evidence presented in the report. Disputes regarding different versions of the incident will be noted and resolved where possible. If the conclusion indicates a violation of the department's policy, the investigator should identify the rule(s), orders, or directives that have been violated.

Recommendations: Some correctional agencies including sheriff's departments do not want the investigator to submit recommendations. If your agency does require recommendations to be included in the report they should be the last part of your report. Before making recommendations, review your agency's policy to determine if there were any policy or procedure violations. If so respectfully recommend the progressive disciplinary action for violation of the applicable policy violated. If your findings conclude that changes should be made to the operational inmate activities schedule to prevent a similar incident from occurring articulate in detail with your recommended changes.

According to the inmate handbook are there any inmate rule violations? If so, ensure that inmate disciplinary action forms (infractions/rule violation reports) are completed by staff and state if your investigation reveals that there are any additional rule violations that should go before the disciplinary board. In case of violations of state or local laws you may recommend a follow-up investigation by your internal affairs unit or local law enforcement agency for possible criminal prosecution.

Attachments: List the chronologically numbered documents relied upon to corroborate your findings, conclusions and possible recommendations. Listed below as an example is a sample partial list:

Attachments:

Divider #1: Staff participant statements (Incident Reports numbered 1 through 3)

Divider #2: Staff witness statements (Incident Reports numbered 4 through 5)

Divider #3: The inmate participant's statement (attachment 6)

Divider #4: Inmate witnesses statements (numbered 7 through 10)

Format Number 2

Some national prisons and juvenile detention centers prefer using a different format on agency letterhead (To, From, Date, Subject) as follows:

Abstract: Topic sentence detailing the, who, what, when, where, how, and why (and actions taken if applicable)

Investigative Leads:

Identification of victim, name and number

Identification of staff witnesses by name and badge/shield number

    1.
    2.
    3.

Identification of inmate witnesses by name and facility number

    1.
    2.
    3.

Other witnesses identified: support personnel, visitors, contractors and so on

1.
2.
3.

Narrative: Include same information as "body" of the report as listed in format number one.

Summary: An analysis of the findings and conclusions and if a follow-up investigation is required to obtain additional information by the internal affairs unit or others.

Attachments: List in numerical order the attachments submitted as part of the investigation, and that demonstrates that the conclusions drawn and recommendation made follow from the evidence. A partial attachment list is submitted below as an example:

Attachments

1. Staff Participant Use of Force Report
2. Staff Witness of Use of Force Report
3. Inmate Participant Allegation and Statement of Force Used
4. Facility Medical Report of Injuries to Staff Participant and Inmate Involved
5. Copy of Facility 24-hour Video Recording of Housing Unit and Incident
6. Inmate Witness Statement

Format Number Three

According to the National Institute of Corrections (2000), at the conclusion of the investigation, the investigator should submit a written report consisting of an objective investigation which recounts all of the facts of the incident, and a summary of the incident along with conclusions for any allegations and recommendations for further action.

Investigation Report

The first part of the report of investigation should be an objective recounting of all the relevant information disclosed during the investigation, including statements, documents, and other evidence and should contain a complete account of the investigation.

Summary and Conclusions

The investigator should summarize the incident and provide a conclusion of fact as to: who, what, when, where, how, and why. If the conduct of an officer was found to be improper, the report must cite the agency rule, regulation or standard operating procedure which was violated. If the conduct of the inmate was found to be improper, the report must cite the agency inmate rule, regulation or standard operating procedure which was violated. Also, any aggravating or mitigating circumstances surrounding the incident such as failure to train staff, lack of proper supervision, improper classification and so on.

If the investigation uncovers evidence of staff misconduct or violation of inmate rules not revealed in the original incident or complaint, this too must be reported and investigated.

References:

National Institute of Corrections, (11/2000). <u>Internal affairs policy and procedure</u> NIC Information Center, p. 11-44.

Chapter 6

INVESTIGATION OF THE USE
OF PHYSICAL FORCE

Chapter Learning Objectives

- Define physical force
- Define and provide examples of excessive physical force
- List six situations when physical force may be used against an inmate
- State some alternative to attempt to avoid physical force
- State who should submit a written report on the use of force and what information the report should contain
- Discuss what constitutes a good report of investigation on a use of physical force
- Address fundamental questions on the force used
- Evaluate excessive force allegations pursuant to U.S. Supreme Court rulings and U.S. District Court rulings

According to Lyons, (1990), inmates have the right secured by the 8th and 14th Amendments to be reasonably protected from violence and the constant threat of violence. They also have the right to seek damages and injunctive relief in federal court against any corrections employees, correctional agencies and county supervisors responsible for county detention centers for abusing these constitutional guarantees.

Unfortunately, some inmates initiate frivolous lawsuits or simply lie almost daily especially in large city correctional systems, county correctional systems along with privatized correctional systems that have a history of not challenging the law suits because it is not in their financial interest to do so. Some correctional agencies feel that it is best to avoid a trial, subpoenas of management, supervisory and line staff that must be back-filled with overtime, in addition to attorney fees, court costs and other related litigation expenses when they can compensate the inmate for a mere fraction of the cost of a trial. Indeed when inmates know that they are being untruthful and could not survive cross examination at trial usually they will agree to a quick low settlement.

Another reason for the inmates' success when the case does go to court is a lack of proper investigation into allegations of staff brutality. Indeed, a review of the literature shows that the two most inmate litigated concerns are inadequate medical treatment and use of physical force, that is, unnecessary and excessive force. This chapter is proactive in the avoidance of inmate lawsuits for excessive force.

Almost always, it is the lack of quality and integrity of internal investigations that enable the inmates' attorneys to show that an assertion--even if it is false--is highly probable. Inmates do not have to show guilt beyond a reasonable doubt in civil cases, they only have to show that the truth of their contentions is highly probable. Correctional agencies control of the investigative process is essential to counter frivolous and untruthful allegations in lawsuits, agencies must document and justify incidents of force.

Courts have stated that since an employing agency controls its employees-having selected, hired, trained, assigned and supervised them--the agency as well as its employees may be held liable (Fisher, Obrien and Austern, 1987). Inmates often seek a financially responsible defendant under the deep pockets theory or who has the most money to pay for alleged injuries caused by correctional employees.

By thoroughly reading and applying the information in this chapter, it should protect correctional staff and correctional systems against false charges by inmates. Supervisory employees and reviewing managers must be aware of these necessary procedures for careful scrutiny of evidence and documenting incidents involving force.

Not only will this chapter discuss this writer's extensive experience in conducting internal investigations on the use of force but also a number of principles and procedures needed for a productive bias-free investigation as identified by the Southern District Court of New York, that is more evident in year 2015 than in 1987.

Physical Force Defined

Physical force in a correctional setting is defined as physical acts deliberately made by an employee with an inmate (or prisoner) in a confrontational situation to control the inmate's behavior or to enforce a lawful order. The physical contact may include offensive or defensive placement of a staff member's hands on an inmate, the application of physical punches, the use of chemical agents such as pepper spray, mace and so on. Or, the use of a weapon such as a side-handled baton (PR 24) riot baton, or the use of mechanical restraints including a restraint chair or restraint belt to cause an inmate to follow any lawful order involuntarily or gain compliance with lawful orders.

Examples of Excessive Force

Some examples of excessive force that New York State courts have identified and based upon this writer's experience includes the following:

- Striking and kicking an inmate when applying arm and body holds would have been adequate to restrain the inmate.
- Punching an inmate when the "simple laying on of hands" (court terminology) or a simple push or shove from one or

more officers would suffice to achieve the desired result. For example, laying hands on an inmate's arm, to guide or lightly push the inmate into a cell and locking the cell.

- Striking an inmate after the inmate has ceased to offer resistance or continuing to strike or kick an inmate after the inmate has been brought under control.
- Use of a mechanical restraints such as handcuffs, for excessive periods of time in an impermissible manner, such as "hogtying" or deliberately tightening restraints to the point that the skin is broken or circulation is cut off.
- Striking an inmate restrained by a mechanical device who has ceased to officer resistance.
- Striking an inmate with a weapon that has not been authorized by facility policy such as a blackjack or slapjack.
- Intentionally striking an inmate with an authorized defensive weapon, such as a PR 24, riot baton or other baton, in a vital and vulnerable area that has been prohibited by agency policy such as the head, kidneys and genitals except as a last resort where there is no other practical alternative available to prevent serious physical injury to staff, visitors or inmates.
- Using agency prohibited choke holds against an inmate.
- The unauthorized use of chemical agents.

The above list constitutes some examples of excessive force brought out in federal court decisions and should be considered according to your agency's policy and procedure on excessive force and in some states the Correction Law or other prevailing state law that defines excessive force and not taken literally.

Six Situations When Physical Force Is Permissible

Investigators should consult their agency policy and procedure and the prevailing state law to determine specifically in the law and policy when an officer is authorized to use physical force on inmates. Generally speaking, an officer may use physical force on an inmate in the following situations:

1. Officers may use physical force to defend oneself, or to defend another employee, inmate or visitor from a physical attack or from an imminent physical attack.
2. To prevent a serious crime, including riots, major disturbances, escapes, escape attempt, rapes and forcible sodomy.
3. To take an inmate into custody or to effect an arrest when resistance is encountered.
4. To enforce agency rules, regulations, directives and court orders. For example, when an inmate refuses to appear at his trial and the presiding judge issues a "order to produce", stipulating that the detention center must produce the inmate to court using whatever force is reasonable and necessary.
5. To prevent serious damage to county, city or state property.
6. To prevent an inmate from self-harm, for example, preventing an inmate from trying to hang himself.

If physical force is used in any situation that is not spelled out in agency policy or the prevailing state law, the investigator must justify the officer's use of force and specify reasons for the particular force used.

Alternatives to Physical Force

Alternatives to the use of physical force may or may not be available based upon the facts and circumstance of the incident. However, if alternatives were available, the investigator should state the alternatives that could have been tried to avoid a use of force. After all, officers are trained to control inmate behavior through the use of interpersonal communications skills and conflict avoidance skills and to anticipate and defuse potentially volatile situations without resorting to the use of force in the first instance. Challenges and ultimatums only heighten tension, increase an inmate's feeling of being threatened and cause the inmate to act out physically.

Whenever possible an officer should attempt to use alternatives to force. An officer should take time to defuse a volatile situation, and should keep calm and try to minimize the involvement of other inmates by isolating the disruptive inmate if possible. According to Lyons (1990a), the officer should, if possible, attempt the following alternatives:

1. Move deliberately and speak slowly and in a conversational tone so as not to arouse suspicion or escalate the situation.
2. Keep a safe distance to avoid physical contact. Attempt to avoid attack by not approaching the inmate unless there is an emergency.
3. Listen to what the inmate has to say and ask for the inmate's cooperation.
4. Explain the consequences of the inmate's behavior, the inmate's failure to cooperate can result in disciplinary charges, loss of good time, loss of meritorious gain time, criminal charges and so on and could extend the inmate's present incarceration.
5. Request the assistance of a superior officer and other custodial staff as a show of force to help resolve the conflict or obtain the inmate's cooperation through a show of force.
6. You may also ask for the assistance of support personnel that may be in the area, for example, the inmate's counselor, priests or other personnel.

Case in Point: After an inmate finished his one-hour recreation period in disciplinary detention, he refused to lock in his cell without cause or justification. Indeed, the inmate stated, *"I'm tired of being locked in that cell"*. The shift sergeant, lieutenant and the chief of security (major) attempted verbal persuasion to gain compliance to no avail. The supervisors requested permission from this writer to activate the facility emergency response team (CERT) to physically put the inmate into his cell. Prior to granting authorization, I asked the inmate's counselor to talk to him and explain the consequences of his behavior. The counselor was someone whom the inmate respected. Approximately two minutes later the chief of security notified this writer that the inmate voluntarily locked back in his cell and apologized for his actions. It has been this writer's experience with state and federal courts that courts often ask: *"Warden, did your staff exhaust all other alternatives prior to taking CERT in there and using force"?* Also, they ask over and over: *"Warden could you have done anything else but use force?* Imagine the report of investigation that shows that staff used every available alternative to avoid using force including supervisors, support personnel and even clergy. This does not make staff look any less masculine for avoiding physical force and you will also gain the inmate's respect.

Who Should Submit a Use of Force Report

Every employee involved in or present at a use of force, or who witnessed a use of force should be required to prepare a detailed written report concerning the incident prior to the end of the shift unless medically unable to do so. The investigating officer should ensure that the following information is submitted by all staff participants in the use of force incident.

Staff Participant's Report of a Use of Force Incident:

- Date and time of incident
- Identify supervisor notified beforehand if it was possible to do so. Whenever a use of force is "anticipated" and the inmate does not pose an immediate threat a supervisor should have been contacted (alternative to force) and all actions should be under the supervisor's direction. In an emergency or a situation where it is not possible or practical to notify a supervisor, staff should be authorized to use force consistent with agency policy and state law (Lyons, 1990b).
- An employee participating in or witnessing a use of force should also be required by agency policy to immediately notify a supervisor, indicating the date and time of notification.
- The name(s) of the inmate(s) against whom force was used and the facility identification number of the inmate

- The inmate rules of discipline violation and number
- Chronological sequence of events leading up to the incident (this is a stated expectation of the federal court as previously mentioned). These facts form a basis for the investigator to evaluate if alternatives were possible and attempted prior to the use of force. Investigators should beware of staff reports that state that "the incident happened spontaneously" or, "it just happened". The federal court said usually something specific--whether building over a period of time or happening at that exact time triggered the incident. The investigator should find out what that was.
- There should be a description of the incident and the specific force used on what part of the body. This is the who, what, when, where, how, and why of the incident? If the report states that an inmate was "restrained by placing him against the wall" the investigator needs to know specifically how the inmate was restrained. Was he restrained by pinning his arms against his body? Was he placed face first against the wall? Or back first? Also the investigator should obtain more detail when you read, "the inmate assumed a fighting stance". What constitutes a fighting stance, does this mean the inmate put his fist up and started towards the officer simulating a boxer's stance?
- Explanation in detail why force was necessary to control the inmate's behavior, remember facility policy states when force is necessary.
- The officer's report should state other employees and inmates who were present during the incident and/or other staff who assisted (other participants) in using force. The report should state how they participated in the incident and describe the actions of the other assisting participants. As the investigator you need to have a clear picture of what each person involved in the incident was doing throughout the incident. If a report fails to state who the witnesses were or does not mention a key witness (especially a non-biased visitor) this requires an explanation.

- Description of any injuries claimed by the staff participants. Here the officer should describe any injuries and how he received them. The injuries described by the officer or the inmate should be consistent with the medical evidence. If an officer claims that he was attacked by an inmate, is there any medical evidence to corroborate that statement (visible injuries)?
- Description of any injuries sustained by participating inmate(s).

Staff Witnessing a Use of Force Incident: As previously stated, any staff member whether custodial or support personnel who are eyewitnesses to a use of force should also submit a written report. The report should be similar to the participating officer's report in some respects as follows:

- Names of inmates involved
- Sequence of events leading up to the incident witnessed
- Use of any alternatives used by the participating officer(s)
- Description of the incident and the specific force observed by the eyewitness
- Why force was necessary based on observations
- Parts of the inmate's body to which force was applied
- Identification of any other eyewitnesses
- Description of any injuries to staff and inmate participants observed by the eyewitness

Report of Investigation on a Use of Physical Force

A good report of investigation on a use of force or allegation of staff brutality on an inmate should include the information below that is consistent with the U.S. Supreme Court:

- Date and time that the investigator was assigned to investigate the incident or state if one is required to investigate the incident as it comes under one's assigned area of responsibility.

- A chronological account of the actions of all staff and inmate participants in the use of force.
- A list of all witnesses with a summary of their verbal and written statements.
- A statement as to the cause of the incident
- A statement of the consistency of the injuries sustained by both staff and inmates along with the medical evaluation and prognosis including possible medical corroborating evidence. Medical evidence should be weighted equally for inmates and staff.
- A list of any inconsistencies by staff or inmates and resolve inconsistencies if possible using some evidence
- A recommendation for any further reports and who should submit those reports.
- Results of all investigations, inquiries into allegations, statements and facility videos viewed
- A statement of any alternatives that were tried before force was used and any alternatives that should have been used based upon the facts and circumstances outlined in reports received
- Based upon the evidence, a statement of whether physical force was necessary based on the prevailing state law and agency policy and procedure
- A statement on who acted properly or improperly according to agency policy and procedure and the inmate rules of discipline
- A statement of any criminal charges and/or disciplinary charges that should be brought against anyone
- Summary of findings and conclusions supported by available evidence
- Recommendations for changing facility operations schedule, policy and procedure or inmate activities
- Attach to the report of investigation sequentially numbered attachments that includes all reports submitted by staff and inmate participants, eyewitness reports, inmate injury reports, staff Worker's Compensation Notice to Employer of Injury, photocopy or photos of any corroborating

evidence, copies of inmate disciplinary reports, diagrams, and sketches

Address Fundamental Questions

The Southern District Court of New York reminds internal investigators that they must pursue and address the most routine and fundamental questions. These include factual questions such as the identity of the aggressor in a physical altercation and the amount of force actually used. Investigators must also address questions of compliance with agency policy, such as whether alternatives to using force--interpersonal communications skills, requests for a supervisor's assistance and if arm and body holds were attempted first or if a lesser amount of force could have been used.

Lyons (1990) states that when posing fundamental questions the investigator should have a copy of the agency's policy and procedure on the use of force available, the employee's actions should be evaluated based on state law and the formal written policy. Step-by-step, the investigator should record the officer's actions according to the law and agency policy. If the agency's policy on the use of force addresses sequential force techniques (force continuum) that should also be addressed.

Use of force techniques include the application of a combination of blocks or control holds to prevent the inmate from continuing an attack. Control holds include hand and body holds but exclude choke holds. Escalating the amount of force according to the amount of escalated force or resistance exhibited by the inmate may include striking the inmate with one or more blows until the inmate discontinues the attack and is under control.

Employ a chemical agent, namely, pepper spray, mace or other chemical agent authorized by agency policy, issued to staff by the agency and training provided by the agency to staff on the proper use of the chemical agent. Whenever chemical agents are deployed medical attention should be provided as soon as possible after the discharge of the agent to both staff and inmates. Only those staff authorized and trained by the agency should administer chemical agents.

Employ an authorized weapon such as a baton or other weapon authorized by law and the agency and under a supervisor's direction. It goes without saying that only staff authorized and trained by the agency should be allowed to use any weapons. Weapons must only be used in the manner taught and authorized by the law and agency policy. In case of private corrections weapons should only be used as authorized and permitted by law, the corporation and the corporation's liability insurance carrier.

Investigators should be aware of the standards for determining undue force as outlined in the landmark case, Johnson v. Glick (1973), that is often referred to as the precedent even in 2015. The precedent set in Johnson v. Glick referred to as *"Stare Decisis"* in simple terms means that the court precedent in use of force cases in jails and prisons has already been set; therefore, *"Let the decision stand in all similar cases"*. In Johnson v. Glick (1973), the court looked at factors such as the need for the application of force, the relationship between the need for force and the amount used, the extent of the inmate's injuries, whether force was applied in a good faith effort to maintain and restore order or was it used maliciously for the very purpose of causing harm to the inmate.

In conclusion, the facts and findings must show that the amount and type of force used was consistent with the force needed to accomplish the objective under the circumstances. In all cases, force must be used only within the circumstances permitted by law and within agency guidelines. As the investigator you must assume the role of impartial fact-finder and a guardian of the inmate's constitutional rights. Investigations training should be a necessary and permanent element of professional corrections training programs. This should be the common denominator for effective performance and management of safe and secure jails and prisons private and public.

Evaluate Excessive Force Pursuant to U.S. Supreme Court Decisions & U.S. District Court Decisions

Restating Wiley (2011), investigators should scrutinize inmate allegations of brutality with an analytical eye because the least protective constitutional standard provides government officials with a great deal of latitude to explain the appropriateness of the force used in a given case. The investigator's findings and conclusions may suggest that an alleged case of staff brutality on an inmate was an entirely permissible use of force under the U.S. Constitution and agency policy and procedure.

However, a use of physical force against an inmate is not justified in response to mere verbal provocation alone or, the inmate withdraws from the encounter. In regard to Jackson v. Austin (2003), the U.S. District Court in a finding that state correction officers used excessive force to restrain an inmate, the court also found that an officer who did not participate in the altercation was liable for failing to intervene in an attempt to terminate the altercation. In addition, Davis v. Carroll (2005), the U.S. District Court ruled that supervisors and managers may also be liable (vicarious liability--liability upon the supervisor for the actions of subordinates). In re: Davis v. Carroll a deputy warden witnessed the incident of excessive force and took no action to stop it or discipline the officers who were involved.

With regard to the use of pepper spray, Norton v. City of Marietta, (2005), the court noted that several actions must be considered, including how long the inmate was sprayed, whether he was adequately irrigated afterward, and whether the pepper spray was used in a good faith effort to restore order and discipline, or was used maliciously and sadistically for the purpose of causing harm. In Danley v. Allyn (2007), regarding a pretrial detainee's cause of action, to wit, the officers' used excessive force in violation of the 14th Amendment by pepper spraying him in response to a dispute over toilet paper. The court noted that the officers had fair warning that to employ pepper spray as punishment, or for sadistic pleasure of the sprayers as distinguished from what was reasonably necessary to maintain prisoner control was constitutionally prohibited.

In <u>Ziemba v. Armstrong</u> (2006), the U.S. District Court in regards to the Connecticut Department of Corrections decided that a correctional officer engaged in reprehensible conduct by hitting an inmate after the inmate was secured with handcuffs. In <u>Long v. Morris</u> (2007), the district court found that the alleged actions of the deputy violated the inmate's rights under the 8th Amendment. The reason for the finding is the record supported an inference that while the inmate was shackled at the wrist, waist and ankles, the deputy took him to the ground, hit his head on the floor hard enough to require stitches and displaced his collar bone.

History reminds us that the U.S. Constitution, and the Bill of Rights were written in part to protect citizens from institutions. According to Wiley (2011), under U.S. Supreme Court precedents there are four different standards to determine what constitutes a government official's use of excessive force, depending upon all of the facts and circumstances of the case at litigation. These provide a basis for the 4th, 8th, and 14th Amendments to the U.S. Constitution.

1. A pretrial detainee is protected under the 14th Amendment's right to substantive due process, and to violate the constitution the official's use of force must be "conscience-shocking" with two culpability standards set apart from one another depending on whether the situation is an emergency or not. Gifis (1984) defines substantive due process as a phrase first introduced in the 5th Amendment to the U.S. Constitution which provides that: *"Nor shall any person be deprived of life, liberty or property, without due process of law"*. This first applied to the federal government but was later made applicable to the states with the adoption of the 14th Amendment. The constitutional safeguard of substantive due process requires that all legislation be in furtherance of a legitimate governmental

objective or what the court characterizes as *"fundamental rights"*.

2. A sentenced inmate (convict) is protected under the 8th Amendment's cruel and unusual punishment clause and to violate the Constitution the official's force must be used maliciously and sadistically with the very purpose of causing harm.

3. In regard to Johnson v. Glick (1973), the court based a pretrial detainee's right to be free from excessive force from a correctional official on the 14th Amendment's substantive due process protection. Glick held that under the U.S. Supreme Court's closely similar case in the past (precedent), to wit, Roncin v. California (1952), the use of undue force by law enforcement officials deprives the suspect of liberty without due process of law. The decision of the above precedent case determined that because no specific U.S. Constitutional Amendment applies to pretrial detainees, the catch-all protection of substantive due process in the 14th Amendment applies to pretrial detainees' claim of excessive use of force.

Glick held that a plaintiff (inmate) may prove an excessive force claim under the 14th Amendment if the inmate shows "conduct that shocks the conscience". Under Roncin, the court provided a four factor test to assist in determining whether a use of physical force met the conscience shocking standard. In a determination of whether or not the constitutional line has been crossed, a court looks to such facts as: *"the need for the application of force, the relationship between the need and the amount of force used, the extent of injury inflicted, and whether or not force was applied in a good faith effort to maintain order or restore discipline or maliciously or sadistically for the very purpose of causing harm"* *(Roncin, 1952, at 1033).*

The Roncin decision recognized that in aspects of jail management there is a reasonable certainty for the need to use physical force. Supervision by a small number of correctional officers and/or jailers of large numbers of inmates often numbering one officer to sixty or more inmates, not usually the most gentile of men and women, may require and indeed justify the occasional use of a degree of force.

In Whitley v. Alberts (1986), regarding an excessive force case by convicted inmates against prison guards during a prison riot, the court held that to establish the use of physical force was excessive, convicts must show that the use of force constituted an *"unnecessary and wanton infliction of pain"* under the 8th Amendment's cruel and unusual punishment clause. Further, that to meet this standard the convicts must focus on the fourth Glick factor and prove that physical force was used "maliciously and sadistically for the very purpose of causing harm". The court further stated:

"Exactly relevant are such factors as the extent of the threat to the safety of staff and inmates, as reasonably perceived by the responsible officials on the basis of the facts known to them, and any efforts made to temper the severity of a forceful response" (Glick at 1085).

Courts have determined that there are two separate and distinct tests to meet the standard to prove conscience-shocking behavior. In Terrell v. Carson (2006), and Sitzes v. City of West Memphis (2010), courts held that to show conscience-shocking behavior in emergency situations, the plaintiff must show that the law enforcement officials and/or prison officers had an intent to harm unrelated to legitimate purpose of good order and discipline. In non-emergency circumstances, the plaintiff must show not only that the officers' behavior reflected a deliberate indifference, but also that it was *"so egregious, so outrageous, that it may fairly be said to shock the contemporary conscience".*

REFERENCES

Danley v. Allyn, 485 F. Supp. 2d 1260 (N.D. Alabama 2007)

Davis v. Carroll, 390 F. Supp. 2d (D Delaware 2005)

Fisher v. Koehler, District Court, Southern District of New York, 83 civ., 2128 (MEL) 1987

Gifis, S. H. (1984). Law dictionary. New York: Barronʼs Educational Series, Inc.

Jackson v. Austin, 241 F. Supp. 2d 1313 (D. Kansas 2003)

Johnson v. Glick, 1973, 481 F. 2d 1028, 1033 (2nd Cir.) 414 U.S. 1033, (1973)

Long v. Morris, 485 F. Supp. 2d 1247 (D. Kan. 2007)

Lyons, D. P. (1990a), August, Preventive Measures Cut Physical Force Suits, Correction Today, pp. 216.224.

Lyons, D. P. (199b). August, Preventive Measures Cut Physical Force Suits, Correction Today.

Norton v. City of Marietta, Ok, 432 F. 3d 1145 (10th Circuit 2005)

Obrien, E., Fisher M. & Austern, D. (1981). Practical law for correctional personnel. Minnesota: West Publishing Co.

Roncin v. California, 342 U.S. 165, 1952

Sitzes v. City of West Memphis, 606 F.3d 461 (8th Cir.) (2010)

Terrell v. Carson, 396 F. 3d 975 (8th Cir.) (2005)

Whitley v. Albers, 475 U.S. 312, (1986)

Wiley, G. (2011), Excessive force claim: disentangling constitutional standards. Bench & Bar of Minnesota. (The Official Publication of the Minnesota State Bar Association)

Ziemba v. Armstrong, 433 F. Supp. 2d 248 (D. Conn. 2006)

Chapter 7

INVESTIGATION OF INMATE ESCAPES FROM FACILITIES

Chapter Learning Objectives

- Discuss the importance of immediate notifications to all concerned personnel especially outside law enforcement authorities
- Explain the reasons for immediate confiscation of log books in the area of concern
- Describe the importance of information gathering
- Explain the value of photographic evidence
- State the information that should be included in the report of investigation into the escape

---

Immediate Notifications to Agency and Outside Law Enforcement Authorities

When the investigator receives notification after business hours that there has been an escape from a detention center or prison one of your first tasks should be to ensure that the shift supervisor has activated the emergency plan for escapes. This includes notifications to outside law enforcement agencies such as the local police, county sheriff and depending on the location, the state police. The facility escape plan should also state that photographs of all of the inmates that escaped should be reproduced so that law enforcement personnel patrolling the area will be able to quickly identify the escapees. Law enforcement personnel should patrol areas of the city and county to recapture the inmates. Shift supervisors or if relieved by the Chief of Security (Incident Commander) or higher authority should go down the list of tasks and responsibilities to be performed after an escape. This is one of the items that will be included in the report of investigation, that is, was the escape plan activated and strictly complied with.

Case in Point #1: Upon notification of an escape, I responded immediately to the facility only to find out that the escape plan had not been activated by the Shift Supervisor or the Chief of Security. Local law enforcement personnel were not notified of the escape until I ordered that the escape plan be activated. A responding city police officer later reported that had the 911 operator been notified on the date and time that the facility became aware of the escape there was a strong possibility that the escaping inmates could have been captured in that an officer was patrolling in the vicinity of the detention center and observed several males running together down the street and disappeared behind a building.

Case in Point #2: In another situation it was reported in a local newspaper that an escape occurred in the local detention center. Law enforcement personnel were not notified immediately, in fact they were not notified until a day and a half later because the detention center tried to recapture the escapees based upon contacts revealed in the inmate record. The Chief of Police was highly upset stating that had 911 been notified they may have been able to apprehend the escapees who were facing murder and armed robbery charges. Additionally, detention center personnel are not trained in law enforcement tactics and techniques and could have been seriously injured on the street trying to recapture the escapees. The Chief also stated that whenever there are dangerous fleeing felons who pose a serious threat to citizens and witnesses, the police have an immediate need to know.

Indeed some jurisdictions require notification to local residents who live in neighborhoods around detention centers and prisons through various means such as a Community Alert Network (recorded telephone notifications to residents of an escape). The recorded message also advises residents to be on the lookout for the escapees, not to approach them but call the police and secure their homes and vehicles.

The emergency plan should also state that once the shift supervisor has been notified of an escape no one enters or leaves the facility, lockdown the entire facility and conduct a census verification (count with inmate photographs). Officers who supervise work crews should return inmates immediately to housing units and account for all tools. Off-duty personnel may be summoned to the facility and the entire facility and the grounds should be searched to ensure that the inmate(s) are not hiding out or waiting for the search to end. Staff may report that inmates have not penetrated the secure barriers confining them at the facility; therefore, they have not escaped. However, if the inmate is not in staff custody, staff do not exercise control over the inmates, then they are not in custody, and has in fact escaped.

If deadly physical force was used to prevent/terminate the escape local law enforcement personnel should be notified (they will notify the medical examiner). We will discuss in-custody deaths in Chapter 9. The investigator should find out if the officer was properly qualified and authorized to use the firearm that caused the death and determine if the officer's actions were pursuant to agency policy and state law. If a firearm was used by the officer the objective of discharging the firearm should be as instructed at the agency firearms academy.

If inmates are apprehended, all individuals and agencies previously notified of the escape should be contacted and informed that the escapees are presently in custody. If facility staff apprehend the inmate(s), Miranda Warnings should be given prior to the investigator questioning the inmate(s).

Confiscation of Log Books

When I am notified of an escape, upon arrival at the facility not only do I go immediately to the escape policy and procedure and the escape plan to ensure tasks and responsibilities listed have been carried out, I also visit the area of escape and confiscate all area log books or other chronological security records where the escape occurred. It is important for the investigator to determine if staff made required security inspections (rounds) as required by policy. This will assist the investigator in analyzing any staff performance issues and recommend the appropriate corrective action. Later on when I get a chance to review chronological security records such as log books I look for squeezed in entries, white out, smeared entries difficult to read, erasure marks, changes in original entries and so on as previously discussed that may suggest that security records have been tampered with in an attempt to cover up the fact that security inspections were not conducted as required.

Information Gathering

Prior to the investigator's arrival the crime scene should have been secured as discussed in Chapter 2, if not, the investigator should ensure that area supervisors follow the institutional policy and procedure on crime scene and evidence preservation. In the absence of a facility policy, follow the guidelines in Chapter 2. After the escapees have been verified through census (picture head count) the investigator should review the inmates' detention/prison record to find all relevant pertinent information about the inmates, for example: possible codefendants, inmates' visitors (visitor list), and so on.

The investigator should supervise officers as they inventory and pack all of the personal property in the inmate(s)' escapee(s)' housing unit. The investigator should carefully go through the inmates' property for any available pre-planning information, evidence or clues to his/her destination. The investigator should also try to determine why inmates selected a certain day or time. For example, one inmate apprehended reported that he selected Saturday nights, midnight shift because the officer steadily assigned to the unit always went into the officer's toilet and slept for hours only waking when he knew the time that the night supervisor would return to make his security rounds.

Peruse the escapee's personal mail in their cell/room for possible clues, that is, information regarding the escape, possible outside accomplices, possible destination or other information.

Value of Photographic Evidence

Photographs are essential in permanently documenting the escapee's route. Photos accurately preserve the scene for possible prosecution and as a proactive strategy to prevent others from escaping via the same means and methods. Pictures should be taken immediately after the escape and before maintenance personnel begin making emergency repairs. "Photographs are highly effective visual aids that corroborate the facts presented" (Hess and Orthmann, 2010, p. 44). Photographs should be taken of the entrance point of the escape and the area leading to and including the exit point. This will reconstruct the avenue of escape. Take both a long range shot of the exit point and a close-range shot of the exit point. Since one of the disadvantages of photographs is that they do not show specific size measurements the investigator may use a marker in the photograph to show the measured size. For example, if an inmate broke through a hole in a wall, a long-range and a close-range photograph of the hole and in a second close-range photograph place a measuring device along side the hole to show the actual size of the hole that the inmates went through.

Garrett (2004), reports that digital cameras are efficient and cost effective for photographing crime scenes. Garrett also states that there are several benefits to using the digital camera including the fact that the photograph is available for immediate viewing and printing if one has the software to do so which includes enlarging the photo. Photographs of other officers on the scene walking around detracts from the purpose of the photograph and brings questions as to the contamination of evidence prior to photographing. "The photos taken could be construed as not an accurate representation of the scene as it was prior to being disturbed" (McAuliffe, 2002, p. 46).

Information That Should Be Included in Report of Investigation

All aspects of the escape should be analyzed and reported using the following according to the chronological order of the investigation:

- When did the escape occur?
- When was it discovered?
- When was it reported?
- Where did the escape occur?
- Where was any evidence found (photographs taken, chain of custody started)?
- Where is the evidence safeguarded?
- Where were the escapees and/or witnesses assigned (housing unit)?
- Who is the escapee or escapees (name, facility identification number, original criminal charges and so on)?
- Who are accomplices (name, ID number, original criminal charges and so on)?
- Who were the staff on duty at the time of the escape?
- Who did the investigator interview and/or interrogate and a brief statement as to the statements made by the interviewee or person interrogated, inconsistencies in statements and the investigator's attempt to resolve inconsistencies?
- Who are possible staff and inmate witnesses?
- Who reported the escape?
- Who received, marked and safeguarded evidence?
- Who was notified (within chain of command and outside law enforcement officials)?
- Who, if any, staff reported any missing tools, date, time and efforts to recover tools?
- Who viewed 24-hour video recordings of the area and state what the video showed?

- What is the approximate amount of damage to facility property (include supporting photographs or sketches)
- What happened, this is the narrative of the actions of perpetrators (escapees), staff and witnesses?
- What preventive measures have been taken?
- What preventive measures are recommended to prevent future escapes?
- What, if any, knowledge, skill, tool(s) etc. was needed to facilitate the escape?
- What important spontaneous declarations (excited utterances) did anyone make regarding the escape?
- What corroborating evidence supports the investigator's findings and conclusions?
- What, if any, further information is needed?
- What further action is needed (e.g. fingerprints, blood analysis etc.)
- Why was a certain day of the week, time of night or shift chosen for the escape?
- Why was certain tools or property stolen
- How was the escape discovered?
- How does this escape relate to any other previous incident at the facility?
- How did the escape occur?
- How were tools used to facilitate the escape?
- How was evidence recovered?
- How was information on the escape obtained?

REFERENCES

Garrett, R. (2004). Is it time to solve the digital mystery? Law Enforcement Technology, February

Hess, K.M. & Orthmann, C.H. (2010). Criminal investigation (9th ed.). Delmar, Cengage Learning, Clifton, New York.

McAuliffe, J. (2002). Criminal investigations. A scenario-Based Text for Police Recruits and Officers, New Jersey: Prentice Hall

Chapter 8

INVESTIGATION OF INMATE RIOTS AND MAJOR DISTURBANCES

Chapter Learning Objectives

- List environmental factors that create tension and inmate unrest as causal factors of riots and major disturbances
- Define a precipitating event
- List and discuss the five stages of a riot
- List implementation strategies to prevent future riots
- Discuss the report of investigation

Let me begin this chapter by stating that in almost all jurisdictions, when a major riot occurs the individual appointed by the facility to conduct the internal investigation will be doing a preliminary investigation. Large detention facilities may request the department's internal affairs unit conduct the investigation. State and/or local law enforcement personnel will probably be called in to do the investigation for prosecutors, mayors, county board of commissioners/supervisors and others who have the management authority over the detention center or prison to obtain an objective assessment of the cause and for prosecution. A law enforcement investigation will take priority if there are deaths of inmates, staff, or civilian hostages. If there is property damage only private prisons will more than likely dispatch their corporate chief internal affairs investigator to the scene as soon as possible to conduct the investigation for the corporation and for corporate insurance purposes. With regard to rural jails, the sheriff most likely will request his law enforcement detective investigator to investigate the incident without using the detention center internal investigator. Or, the sheriff may request an investigator from the state police. Prior to the facility investigator attempting to investigate a riot or major disturbance he/she should have some knowledge of riots and major disturbances especially when formulating causal factors, analyzing the actions of all concerned according to established policy and state law and forming factual findings and conclusions.

Even when conducting only a preliminary investigation into a riot, the investigator should uncover a large amount of data. Many questions must be answered as we will discuss later on in this chapter. As previously stated in Chapter 5, prior to writing the report of investigation, I respectfully recommend obtaining a one-quarter inch or larger three-ring binder depending upon the anticipated volume of data expected to be collected, a three-hole punch and dividers will also be useful for the attachments to your report. The inmate and staff reports along with sketches, photographs and other data accumulated as attachments will be organized in the binder in chronological order of the investigation beginning with the reason you are investigating the incident and ending with factual findings, conclusions supported by evidence and recommendations.

Environmental Causes of Riots and Major Disturbances

There may not be a single cause of a riot or major disturbance that would fit every prison or detention center. Riots may arise due to real or inmate perceived civil rights violations, totality of conditions of confinement that may or may not have been ignored by the administration. Seiter, (2011), reports on one of the most serious riots in 1971, at the state prison in Attica, New York (Attica Riot) that tensions had begun building for several months as inmates repeatedly complained to the administration and even wrote the governor regarding poor food, inadequate medical care and discrimination by staff requesting more African-American and Hispanic staff since most of the inmates were black and Hispanic. Prior to the riot most staff were Caucasian. After the New York State Police retook the prison after four days 32 inmates and 11 staff were found dead. According to the American Correctional Association (1990), some contributing environmental factors that create tension and inmate unrest that could lead to riots and major disturbances are as follows:

- Security threat groups, the gangs often try to prove that they are in fact running the detention center or prison and challenge the authority of the administration.
- Limitations on inmate movement and freedoms
- Inmate perceived staff brutality condoned by the administration, 8th and 14th Amendment violations (as previously stated one of the leading causes of inmate litigation)
- Racial conflicts usually between African-Americans and Hispanics
- Overcrowded living conditions for example, a housing unit designed for 30 inmates but actually confining 60 or more inmates and/or crowded conditions causing inmates to sleep in hallways and gymnasiums.
- Real or perceived staff indifference to adequate medical care
- Inmate allegations of inadequate portions of food, poor quality, no fresh fruits or vegetables and/or not enough variety in food.
- Inappropriate and inadequate staffing to protect inmates. Inmates seem to have a keen interest in the administration providing sufficient numbers of staff to provide basic safety and life safety issues for inmates. Case in Point: In one large detention center that I worked in the inmates put in a grievance to the commissioner of correction that there should be two officers assigned to housing units on the 12 midnight to 8 AM shift instead of one officer responsible for 120 inmates. The inmates stated that if that one officer had a heart attack or some other medical crisis and passed out

there was no other officer in the housing unit to prevent/ terminate and inmate suicide or to unlock cells in case of a fire.
* Inequality of the criminal justice system based on race including courts, probation and parole.

In addition to the environmental factors reported by the ACA, Seiter (2011) includes the following:

* Hot weather especially during summer months in facilities without air conditioning
* Reduction in budgets for recreational equipment
* Perceived patterns of unfairness of prison management
* Poor security procedures that allow inmates to create an unsafe environment

Precipitating Event

Seiter (2011), defines a precipitating event as the *"spark in the haystack"*. Stinchcomb & Fox (1999), reports that inmates may peacefully exist in what they perceive as negative environmental conditions. However, at some point an unexpected unanticipated event may cause an eruption of a massive violent response. Some abrupt altercation between officers and inmates, a brief and unexpected breach of security that becomes a foiled escape attempt and so on. Stinchomb & Fox (1999), also report that a publicized account of events outside the detention center or prison can serve as a precipitating event, as occurred with federal immigration actions that caused the Atlanta and Oakdale riots of 1987.

Based upon this writer's experience inappropriate classification decisions can also serve as a precipitating event. Case in Point: At a large detention center two super max inmates were transferred from super max to another housing unit classified medium custody as a result of being incorrigible management problems that could not get along with other similarly classified super max inmates. The inmates should have been transferred to administrative segregation or transferred to another facility similarly classified super max. After being transferred to medium custody, the inmates were very angry and intimidated the medium custody inmates who previously had not voiced any complaints with the administration. The newly assigned super max inmates attempted to escape through a window but when the escape was foiled they told the other inmates "either you fight the police or you fight us". In brief, 120 inmates took the three housing unit officers hostage, tied them up, beat one officer severely, set fires, flooded the unit, damaged the housing unit, made weapons with mop wringers, mop sticks, placed pillow cases over their heads and began to riot. A facility response team discharging multiple rounds of CS and CN gas freed the hostages and restored control and order in the housing unit.

Five Stages of a Riot

Criminal Justice experts Stinchomb and Fox (1999), state that generally riots tend to proceed in five stages:

1. **Initial Explosion**: that is, the spontaneous or in some cases planned uprising during which inmates gain control of all or various sections of the institution.
2. **Organization:** inmate leadership comes into existence.
3. **Confrontation:** inmates are confronted either by the staff use of physical force, deadly physical force or negotiation.
4. **Termination:** Custodial control and good order is restored through physical force, deadly physical force or negotiation
5. **Explanation:** this is the who, what, when, where, how, why and what actions were taken or in other words the investigation

Some Strategies to Prevent Future Riots

I have provided below an example of some strategies that the investigating officer can use as recommendations to prevent a recurrence of riots depending upon all the facts and circumstances of a particular riot and strategies of the U.S. Department of

Justice. Also included are strategies from the National Institute of Justice, Research Brief, October (1995), after probably the most investigated riot in U.S. history, namely, the Southern Ohio Correctional Facility riot in rural Lucasville, the riot lasted eleven days in which one officer and nine inmates were murdered, and thirteen officers were taken hostage.

- If activities schedules, policies or procedures was a causal factor the policies and procedures should be reviewed, revised and/or new policies implemented.
- Staff training may be expanded, enhanced and updated.
- An inmate grievance resolution program may be implemented where the facility management and inmate nominated spokespersons sit down at a table once monthly to discuss any environmental factors or totality of conditions of confinement and try to resolve issues peacefully. Additionally, inmates who have grievances should write them on the designed form and present them to elected inmate grievance representatives to be resolved informally or resolved at the monthly grievance resolution committee meeting.
- Formulate a strategic threat group (gang) management intelligence gathering and reporting and classification system
- Maximum security inmates should be single celled and appropriately classified. Special trained officers should be assigned to maximum security housing units.
- Staffing numbers should be consistent with required Human Resource staffing requirements and contractual obligations (privatized prisons) for the safety and security of the facility.
- If possible, avoid budget cuts in areas of life safety issues, good order, safety and security of the institution.
- Stay abreast of the current state of the art technology in riot control techniques, equipment and training.
- Correctional staff should receive annual in-service training to recognize the early warning signs that inmates may be planning to riot.

- Facility administrators should get out of their offices on a regular basis and away from computers and practice *"Management by Walking Around"* so that they are accessible to inmates and staff and so that their education and years of experience will enable them to recognize predisposing conditions that could lead to a riot and security breaches (Lyons, 1992).
- The chief of security or higher ranking manager should perform security audits to ensure that staff remain in compliance with all security and control policies and procedures and safety and emergency procedures. This allows the facility to discover deficiencies before exploited by inmates.
- The chief of security or security captain should closely monitor tool control and accountability and contraband control to prevent inmates from possessing unauthorized tools, storing excessive amounts of commissary items and search and control of contraband especially inmate homemade weapons.
- Strict enforcement of inmate discipline. If inmates see that staff do not care or cannot protect them, they will make weapons and protect themselves.

Physical Force Issues

Investigators should refer to Chapter 6, of this book regarding the investigation of physical force. In most cases specially trained prison/detention center personnel (Correction Emergency Response Teams) will terminate riots and major disturbances with facility personnel as support (escort to medical clinic, local hospital, placement in administrative segregation and so on). In rural jurisdictions the sheriff's trained law enforcement riot control team will respond or the local city police emergency response/ tactical response units. When the decision is made by appropriate authority to use physical force to terminate the riot and restore order and discipline, the type of force and level of force to be used will be dictated by the situation. Multiple squads of uniformed staff (support) should be deployed from different directions and in adequate numbers to assure that rioting inmates do not overcome the tactical groups.

Report of Investigation

At the conclusion of any law enforcement investigation the facility investigator should be assigned to conduct an extensive investigation from a correctional standpoint, namely, policy, procedures, security, inmate discipline violations and to make recommendations to prevent recurrence. The investigation should answer the following questions using the same who, what, when, where, how, why, and what actions taken format in chronological order of investigative procedures and techniques:

- Date and time of incident and who (or policy/post requirement) assigned the investigator to the investigation and reporting.

WHO?

- reported the incident?
- was notified?
- were the inmate rioters (participants) witnesses, inmates who refused to take part in the riot?
- was interviewed and submitted written reports including rioters and instigators, and staff?
- if any, who were the inmate(s), staff, or visitor(s) hostages?
- gave the order to use physical force or deadly physical force?
- was the police official or correctional official that gave the required Miranda Warnings to rioters who will be charged with violations of law?
- were all the staff participants and/or witnesses involved in the incident?
- made any significant spontaneous declarations (excited utterances) about the riot?

- was injured during the riot both staff and inmates and any others whether or not they received or refused medical treatment?
- were the inexperienced officer(s) participants who may not have known how to manage prisoners (new probationary officers)?
- set- up a security perimeter outside and possibly surrounding the facility in order to secure the outside perimeter and prevent escapes during the riot (police officials or correctional staff)?
- were the staff members that video recorded the riot?
- marked and received any evidence?
- were the outside responding medical support personnel that may have rendered medical triage and emergency first aid?
- if any, who were the hostage negotiators used?

WHAT?

- were the inmate alleged environmental causes and precipitating events leading to the riot?
- were the specific actions of identified rioting inmates?
- were the specific actions of staff including facility emergency response team personnel?
- were the demands of the hostage takers in order to free hostages if applicable?
- were the extent of injuries of all concerned?
- were the specific crimes committed and violations of inmate rules of discipline?
- is the damage to institutional property?
- happened, that is, the narrative of the actions of all concerned?
- evidence was recovered?
- preventive measures if any, had been taken to prevent riots?
- statements were made and by whom?
- further information is needed if any?
- further action is needed, if any?

- type of force was used including: riot batons, pepper spray, mace, CN or CS gas and so on. If gas was used, in what quantities were they used in various areas? In an inmate lawsuit inmates' attorneys may question why excessive chemical agents was used in an area that training in chemical agents mandate that for the square footage only "X" amount of chemical agents (CN or CS) should have been used for life safety reasons and excessive amounts were used for the stated square footage to punish inmates.

WHEN?

- as previously stated, date and time of incident?
- were notifications up the chain of command made as well as to outside agencies such as law enforcement officials?
- was the incident reported?
- was the tactical response team dispatched to the scene?
- was good order, security and discipline restored (conclusion of riot)?
- did the investigator review CERT videos of actions taken during the riot and the facility 24-hour video of the housing unit and what did the video show?
- were hostages released if applicable?

HOW?

- was the riot discovered?
- does this incident relate to any other recent incident at the facility?
- was evidence discovered and marked for possible criminal prosecution?
- was information and/or intelligence obtained?
- many staff and inmate participants were involved in the riot?
- long did it take to bring the riot under control?
- many inmates and staff had to be transferred to an outside hospital (identify them)?

- many inmates and/or staff were admitted to the hospital (identify them)?
- were hostages released if applicable?
- were the perpetrators escorted throughout the facility at the conclusion of the riot (gauntlet, under supervision of officers and a supervisor, escorted by CERT, etc.)?(Note: prior to being escorted from the scene did the inmates have any noticeable injuries but upon arrival to destination had newly visible injuries)?
- was the area secured at the conclusion of the riot?

WHY?

- was a particular date, time or shift selected?
- were the named rioters transferred to other institutions or temporarily reclassified?
- did the riot occur?

REFERENCES

American Correctional Association (1990), Causes, preventive measures, and methods of controlling riots and disturbances in correctional institutions, pp. 8-13, Laurel, MD

Lyons, D. P. (1992, April), Management by Walking Around (M.B.W.A.). Keepers Voice, pp. 14-15, Volume 13, Number 2.

Seiter, R. P. (2011). Corrections and introduction (3rd ed.). New Jersey: Pearson Education, Inc.

Stinchcomb, J.B. & Fox, V.B. (1999). Introduction to corrections. (5th ed.). New York: Prentice Hall, Inc.

U.S. Department of Justice, National Institute of Justice, Research Brief, October 1995, Bert Useem, Camille Graham Camp, G. M. Camp, and Renie Dugan. Resolution of prison riots.

Chapter 9

INVESTIGATION OF IN-CUSTODY DEATHS

Chapter Learning Objectives

- Discuss the two primary causes of jail suicides
- List and discuss suicide attempt/post suicide procedures according to national standards
- Consistent with national standards, differentiate the two levels of supervision generally recommended for suicidal inmates
- Discuss the elements of an effective suicide prevention plan according to national standards
- List and discuss the information that should be included in the preliminary investigation of a suicide
- Define positional asphyxia
- Discuss the pre-disposing factors in positional asphyxia
- Discuss preliminary investigation of positional asphyxia

Although this is not a course on suicideology there is some basic information that institutional investigative supervisors conducting basic suicide investigations should know, and reviewing managers should know. But before getting started and as previously discussed law enforcement officials including state bureaus of investigation and the county or city medical examiner/coroner will take the lead in this type of investigation. Indeed, in some jurisdictions a medical examiner's inquest is mandatory with relation to inmate suicides. The medical examiner will be the one who determines the cause of death and will schedule an autopsy. According to Hayes and Rowan (1988), suicides is the leading cause of death in jails nationally. Pearson, Peltz and Shafner (2014), provide an important clue for investigators to be on the lookout for, that is, safeguards designed to prevent inmate suicides may not be followed by staff which is a contributing factor for jail suicides and may subject the correctional agency to a wrongful death lawsuit.

Based on this writer's experience, some other clues that investigators should be on the lookout for is breakdowns in communication between mental health staff and custodial personnel, improper or no documentation in record keeping, inadequate or no mental health treatment especially in rural jails and lockups. In some rural jails and lockups generally new admission prisoners are not screened by medical or mental health staff and are normally classified as part of the general inmate population by intake officers or deputy jailers.

Two Primary Causes of Jail Suicides

Rowan and Hayes (1995), state that the number of jail suicides far exceeds the number of prison suicides. Indeed, the U.S. Bureau of Justice Statistics (1993), reports that suicide ranks third as a cause of death in prisons. Rowan and Hayes list two primary causes for jail suicides as environment and inmates facing crisis situations. Rowan and Hayes (1995), report that from the inmate's perspective certain features of the jail environment enhance suicidal behavior, that is, fear of the unknown, distrust of the authoritarian environment, perception of lack of apparent control over the future, isolation from family and significant others, shame of being incarcerated and the perceived dehumanizing aspects of incarceration. Factors often found in inmates facing a crisis situation that could predispose inmates to suicide are recent excessive consumption of alcohol and/or use of drugs, severe guilt or shame over the offense that they have been charged with and current mental illness and/or prior history of suicidal behavior.

Rowan and Hayes report that these factors become exacerbated during the first 24 hours of incarceration when the majority of jail suicides occur.

The research of Rowan and Hayes (1995), also shows that victims of suicide had a documented history of diagnosed mental illness or treatment, had attempted suicide before or made suicidal gestures in the past. Facility policy should affirmatively state that staff have a responsibility for preventing suicides through intake screening, identification and supervision of suicide prone inmates. At the academy, all custodial staff should have received special training in the recognition of suicide prone inmates, suicide prevention and first aid and cardio pulmonary resuscitation (CPR). Investigators should be aware of staff reports that state that they cut an inmate down from hanging and stood around awaiting the arrival of facility medical personnel or outside emergency medical technicians who could be tied up on other medical emergencies. Upon the arrival on the scene of a possible suicide, officers should not presume that the inmate is already deceased but rather initiate and continue CPR. Staff trained in 1st Aid/CPR should administer it until the arrival of medical personnel. Failure to administer CPR in a timely manner may be one of the contributing factors of death.

Suicide Attempt/Post Suicide Procedures

Once outside emergency medical technicians or the medical examiner pronounce the inmate as dead on arrival officers should treat the possible suicide as a possible homicide until informed to the contrary by the medical examiner/coroner or law enforcement personnel. This means safeguarding any possible suicide notes, and treating the areas as a crime scene (preservation of crime scene). Listed below consistent with the National Commission on Correctional Health Care (NCCHC) (1992), are the duties and responsibilities of the first officer to arrive on the scene of a suicide attempt or suicide:

First Officer on Scene

Immediately call for assistance of other staff.

Get the victim down if hanging

Second Officer on Scene

Request facility medical personnel or if unavailable request the assistance of outside emergency medical technicians.

Assist with CPR as necessary

Maintain security and preserve scene as much as possible

A logbook should be maintained of anyone entering or leaving the scene and what time they entered and departed. The area should remain secured until the Medical Examiner or law enforcement personnel release the scene.

Your investigation should show whether or not officers followed suicide protocol as listed in facility policy and had the required equipment available to them to be used in case of suicide as should be stated and required by agency policy and explanations as to whether or not the equipment was used in responding to the suicide. If the required equipment was not available to staff and not required by policy and procedure, the investigator should make a recommendation that the below equipment should be made available to staff according to national standards of the ACA and the NCCHC.

Required Equipment

Airway protective service
Surgical gloves
Blood stopper compression bandage
Hoffman design 911 rescue tool (special security knife)

Pocket mask
Bite block

Levels of Supervision for Possible Suicidal Inmates

According to Hayes (1994) and consistent with national standards generally there are two levels of supervision recommended for suicidal inmates: 1.) close observation and 2.) constant observation. Close observation is for inmates not actively suicidal but expresses suicidal ideation and/or has a recent history of self destructive behavior. Officers should observe the inmate at irregular intervals not to exceed 15 minutes. Inmates who actively pose a suicidal risk by either threatening self-destructive behavior or engaging in the suicidal behavior should have constant observation. Staff should observe inmates on constant observation on a continuous, uninterrupted basis either by direct visual observation, through the use of closed circuit television or in some large detention facilities inmate suicide aides/monitors. Inmate suicide aides are volunteers trained by the correctional agency in suicide recognition and prevention and assists officers in preventing suicides. Normally the aides receive a small credit in the facility commissary (store) for their services. Suicide aides may be used to supplement but "never" a substitute for the observation stated above. If an inmate was on close observation or constant observation as the investigating officer, upon entering the housing unit the first thing I do is confiscate the suicide observation record (form) or other document showing that observation was or was not in fact being carried out.

Other suicide prone inmates require officers to check on their physical well being every 30 minutes to ensure that they are alright (Seiter, 2011). Even with suicide prevention programs in place it may be difficult to prevent. Case in Point: An inmate pulled the sheet and wool blanket up to his neckline then underneath the sheet and blanket he slashed his wrist and bled to death on the midnight shift. The inmate was not on any type of suicide watch and was housed in general population. The midnight shift officer made his rounds as required by policy and reported that the inmate appeared to be sleeping like all of the other inmates with the blanket pulled up to his neckline (winter months). After the inmate did not get up out of bed to receive his food tray at breakfast, the officer went into the cell and tried to awaken the inmate. After he was unable to awaken the inmate the officer pulled back the covers and discovered that the inmate had cut his wrist sometimes during the night or early morning hours.

Elements of an Effective Suicide Prevention Plan

As part of the internal investigation one should compare the agency's suicide prevention plan to the actions or inactions of staff to ensure that it was fully complied with by the staff having supervision over the inmate. If the agency's suicide prevention policy, procedure and plan are not in accordance with the recommended standards of the American Correctional Association and/or the National Commission on Correctional Health Care, the investigator should recommend revisions to the agency policy pursuant to national standards. Analyze, compare and contrast the national standards with the agency plan as a proactive strategy to prevent recurrence. Management of detention centers or prisons without adhering to national standards whether the facility is accredited or not is a disaster just waiting to happen and a haven for inmate lawsuits especially in the area of suicide prevention and wrongful death. Prominent physicians, psychiatrist, correctional managers and attorneys have agreed and wrote the national standards relative to suicide prevention as written in the National Commission of Correctional Health Care and the American Correctional Association Standards of confinement to prevent suicides.

According to the Office of the Correctional Investigator of Canada (2014), the National Commission on Correctional Health Care (1992), and Rowan and Hayes (1988), a comprehensive suicide prevention program should contain the integrated measures and interventions including the following:

<u>Screening, Identification and Assessment of Suicide Risk</u>: The preliminary facility screening form normally conducted by an intake officer should contain observations and interview items relating to the risk of potential suicide. A follow-up screening and assessment should be conducted by mental health professionals as soon as possible who designates the level of suicide risk.

<u>Staff Training in Suicide Awareness and Prevention</u>: This should be part of the officer's initial and annual in-service training curriculum. The training curriculum should be designed according to state mental health, ACA and NCCHC standards.

<u>Protocols for Monitoring and Management of Suicidal Behavior</u>: Facility policy and procedures should specify the facility's procedures for monitoring inmates who have been identified as suicide potentials including regular, documented supervision. Policy and procedure should also specify the procedures for referring suicide potentials to mental health professionals.

<u>Physical Environment</u>: Blind spots in housing areas and/or cell design including metal furniture and fixtures (especially double bunks and sharp edges) identified, removed, and mitigated to the safest extent possible.

<u>Communication</u>: Procedures for information sharing on past or recent behavior of suicidal inmates between custodial staff, medical providers and mental health professionals regarding the status of the inmate to provide clear and current information.

<u>Intervention</u>: Policy and procedure should address how to handle a suicide attempt in progress, including cutting down a hanging inmate and other first aid/CPR measures.

<u>Notifications</u>: Policy and procedures for notifying appropriate facility administrators, outside authorities, family members and other appropriate officials.

<u>Reporting and Review</u>: Appropriate reporting procedures for documenting the identification and monitoring of potential or attempted suicides shall be detailed as procedures for reporting a completed suicide. Additionally, there should be periodic audits of the overall suicide prevention program and strategies to maintain effectiveness of the program.

<u>Critical Incident Stress Debriefing</u>: Crisis intervention and traumatic stress awareness professionals available for both staff and inmates.

Preliminary Internal Investigation

Sample
First Paragraph (Background)

Submitted herein is a report of investigation into the apparent suicide of (<u>inmate's name,and identification number</u>), on (<u>date, time and housing location</u>), discovered by Officer (<u>name and I.D. number</u>), as officer conducted his security rounds he found above inmate hanging in his cell from the top bunk bed frame by a sheet tied around his neck. A suicide note was found laying on the cell table. The note stated that the inmate took his own life because he now comes under the three strikes rule; therefore, if found guilty he will be sentenced to life in prison. Officer (_____) requested immediate assistance over the two-way radio from custodial staff, medical staff and his supervisor. While awaiting arrival of assistance, the officer gently lifted the inmate's legs up to release pressure on the inmate's neck and used his Hoffman 911 Rescue Knife to cut the inmate down then he began CPR. Facility medical personnel notified outside emergency medical technicians who pronounced the inmate dead on arrival. Investigating officer notified the control room supervisor to contact 911 police emergency and the county medical examiner for investigation.

As previously stated, the first paragraph must show: **who, what, when, where, how, why, and what actions taken?**

Secondary Paragraph:

Inmate profile discussing the background of the inmate as documented in the jail/prison record, e.g. date admitted to the facility, details of suicide assessment upon entering the facility, criminal charges, brief history of previous incarcerations and classification, prior medical/mental health issues, substance abuse history and so on.

Third Paragraph:

Investigation - new paragraph for each different subject written in chronological order of events and in narrative form answering in more detail the following questions:

Who? assigned this investigation to you or does it come under your area of responsibility?

was the medical examiner/coroner that responded?

were the law enforcement officials that responded to the scene?

were witnesses, if, any?

answered the officer's call for assistance?

were emergency medical personnel and outside emergency personnel that responded?

confiscated, marked and received evidence (suicide notes, bed sheets etc.)?

What? type of incident occurred?

happened (narrative of the apparent actions of all concerned)?

evidence was found?

further information is needed (autopsy)?

if, any, further action is needed?

When?

did the incident occur?

was it discovered?

was it reported?

Where?

did the incident happen?

was evidence found?

was the evidence stored?

was the victim and/or possible witnesses housed?

How? was the suicide discovered?

did the incident occur?

was evidence found?

Why? did the inmate apparently commit suicide?

why was a particular day or time selected, if known?

Findings and Conclusions (Supported by evidence):

A critical review of all the statements, facts, circumstances and evidence surrounding this incident suggest what?

What Actions Taken if, Any By the Investigating Officer? (notifications made, securing crime scene, etc.)

A critical review of this incident with regard to agency's policies and procedures on suicide prevention program suggest what, if anything?

Possible Answer: An objective review of this agency's suicide prevention policy reveals that it was written according to the suggested guidelines of the ACA and the NCCHC, and the policy has been updated annually. Additionally, the actions of all staff concerned were evaluated according to agency policy and their actions were consistent with tasks and responsibilities required by the suicide prevention program.

A synopsis of training received by facility custodial staff reveal? (what?)

Possible Answer: A review of the academy's training curriculum for correctional officers is consistent with the tasks, responsibilities and guidelines of the ACA and NCCHC as well as the State Department of Mental Health. All staff who work with inmates are thoroughly trained in suicide prevention and evaluated with role play to recognize verbal and behavioral cues that indicate suicide potential. In addition, there is documentary evidence on file in the training office that all staff receive annual in-service training on the suicide prevention program and training objectives are evaluated with a final test in which each learner must receive a minimum grade of 85 percentile.

A review of intake screening, medical and mental health involving the inmate victim suggest? (what)

Possible Answer: A review of the intake screening form contains observation and interview items related to the inmate's potential suicide risk. The form conforms to ACA, NCCHC, and State Mental Health Department guidelines for assessing suicide potential. After the officer prepared the intake screening form the inmate was interviewed by the nurse on duty (Nurse, Jane Doe, RN) and the nurse did not see any valid reason for suicide concerns as stated in her report submitted herein as Attachment 14).

Discuss evidence of a "precipitating factor":

Possible Answer: Available evidence, to wit, inmate statements and suicide note found on the scene suggest that the pre-incident indicator, precipitating event or contributing risk factor that brought the inmate to the decision to take his own life was the conversation he had on the inmate telephone (written transcript of call submitted herein as evidence, Attachment 15), when his wife informed him that upon this new arrest and his looking at a life sentence under the three strike's rule, that she would not wait for him this time, or visit him in prison. She was going to divorce him and meet someone else.

Recommendations (if any):

Some Possible Recommendations

To further indemnify staff and this agency, respectfully recommend that state licensed mental health professionals assisted by custodial training staff teach the suicide curriculum instead of custodial staff alone. Mental health professionals will be able to add a new dimension to the curriculum and answer questions and submit case studies that custodial staff may not be able to do.

Are there any specific recommendations for changes in the agency's suicide prevention program, policy and procedure, physical plant or facility operations?

Does evidence suggest that there should be any changes to the intake screening process or interview questions?

Are there any "best practices" used at other detention facilities that could be incorporated in this facility to prevent suicides?

If, and, only if, staff did not follow suicide policy, so state this violation and any recommended progressive disciplinary actions to prevent recurrence.

Positional Asphyxia

Positional asphyxia is also known as postural asphyxia, and is unconsciousness or death resulting from a lack of oxygen that occurs when someone's position prevents the person from breathing adequately. According to Reay (1996), a significant number of individuals die suddenly during restraint by police officers, positional asphyxia may be a factor in some of the deaths. Correctional officers should also be aware of the possibility of inmate deaths brought on by positional asphyxia when restraining inmates. Positional asphyxia is a potential danger of some physical restraint techniques. Inmates may die from positional asphyxia by simply getting themselves into a breathing restricted position that they cannot get out of (Reay, 1996).

A review of the literature suggests that restraining a person in a face down position is likely to cause greater restriction of breathing than restraining a person face up (Parkes & Carson, 2008; Reay, 1996). Reay (1996) also reports that many law enforcement, corrections and medical personnel are now taught to avoid restraining people face down or to do so only for very short periods of time. Some risk factors that may increase the chance of death includes obesity, prior cardiac or respiratory problems, and the use of illicit drugs such as cocaine (Stratton, Rogers & Gruzaski, 2000). Parkes and Carson (2008), state that other issues in the way people are restrained can also increase the risk of death, for example, kneeling or otherwise placing weight on the person and particularly any type of restraint hold around the person's neck. Or, while restraining an inmate who is face down on the floor, an officer places his/her knee in the inmate's back for a period of time in an attempt to calm the inmate down and handcuff him. Parkes and Carson (2008), also report that research measuring the effect of restraint positions on lung functions suggests that restraint which involves bending the restrained subject or placing body weight on them has more effect on their breathing than face down position.

Parkes, Thake and Price (2011), report that positional asphyxia is not limited to restraint in a face down position. Restraining a subject in a seated position could also reduce the ability to breathe if the subject is pushed forward with the chest on or close to the knees. The risk will be higher in cases where the restrained person has a high body mass index and/or large waist girth.

Parkes and Carson (2008), state that resuscitation of persons who exhibit cardiac arrest following restraint has proven to be difficult. Even in cases where the subject was in the immediate care of emergency medical technicians has failed and the person died.

Predisposing Factors to Positional Asphyxia

In addition to the factors listed by Stratton, Rogers, & Gruzaski (2001), the National Law Enforcement Technology Center (1995), reports some other factors that may render some people more susceptible to positional asphyxia following a violent struggle particularly when the subject is in a face-down prone position are as follows: Obesity as previously stated, alcohol and high drug use, and an enlarged heart "renders an individual more susceptible to a cardiac arrhythrnia under conditions of low blood oxygen and stress" (p. 2). Additionally, the risk of positional asphyxia is compounded when the person with predisposing factors becomes involved in a violent struggle with officers especially when physical restraint includes the use of rear handcuffing combined with placing the person on his stomach.

Internal Preliminary Investigation of Positional Asphyxia

In regard to any in-custody death, local law enforcement officials will be called after emergency medical technicians pronounce the inmate as deceased. Law enforcement personnel should notify the county or city medical examiner/coroner who will conduct his/her independent investigation involving forensic technology. Usually the facility internal investigator will be asked to conduct the internal preliminary investigation not for forensics but for policy, procedure and security concerns. The facility investigation should determine the facts and circumstances as to how the inmate died as verified by the medical examiner, any staff that possibly contributed to the death, and were policies on the use of force complied with regarding restraint techniques.

If the investigator is lucky there will be a 24-hour facility security video recording of the entire incident and/or a facility emergency response team video for the investigator to view and analyze according to policy and procedure requirements. After gathering all of the use of force reports and staff and inmate witness statements the investigator should look for corroborating evidentiary statements of how the inmate was restrained. The critical question to be pursued is, was the inmate restrained pursuant to agency policy, procedure and staff training on restraint techniques. If the answer is "yes", staff should be indemnified by the agency in case of a wrongful death law suit. However, if the answer is "no", that staff did not follow policy and training on restraint techniques and this ultimately contributed to the inmate's death the investigator's report should so state with detailed information along with a copy of the facility video recording as documentary evidence. If the investigator's report does not reflect the truth of the matter or withholds critical evidence such as video recordings, I can guarantee you that the inmate's attorney will request to view any such videos and when the truth comes out, the investigator may be accused of a cover-up and a failure to conduct a proper investigation.

Investigators should use the counter on the video recorder or video player to try and determine how long the inmate was involved in a violent struggle resisting officers especially when the physical restraint included the use of rear handcuffing combined with placing the inmate on his stomach or restraining the inmate in a seated position so as to restrict his ability to breathe. Investigators should review the inmate's record to determine obesity, alcohol, illegal drug use, or the possibility of an enlarged heart as predisposing factors to positional asphyxia. Additionally, if the inmate was transported to an outside medical facility before he became deceased, state in what position the inmate was transported and if possible find out how long the transport lasted and if any unusual observations were recorded by the transporting medical personnel. If possible, obtain a copy of the medical examiner's written report. If this is not possible then obtain an oral statement from the medical examiner regarding the postmortem examination including the nature of injuries, diseases or drugs present in the inmate and any other significant factors that contributed to the death.

If positional asphyxia was in fact the contributing factor to the inmate's demise, the investigator may make recommendations to revise agency policy and training on restraint techniques to prevent this type of incident from reoccurring. The City of New York, Police Department trains police officers in the methods below as a proactive strategy to prevent deaths in custody as follows and these methods may be used by the investigator as part of the investigator's recommendations to prevent reoccurrence:

- As soon as the inmate is handcuffed (usually in the rear), get him off his stomach by placing him on his side or place him in a seated position with nothing obstructing his breathing.
- If the inmate continues to struggle, officers should not sit on his back or place a knee in his back or apply the officer's body weight on the inmate's back. Instead hold his legs down or wrap his legs with a strap.
- Never hogtie and inmate by tying the handcuffs to a leg or ankle restraint
- If the inmate is transported in a facility operated ambulance or other facility vehicle, do not lay the inmate on his stomach while being transported to an outside hospital. Place him in a seated position.

References:

American Correctional Association (1990). <u>Standards for adult correctional institutions</u> (3rd ed.) Laurel, Maryland

Bureau of Justice Statistics (1993). <u>Correctional population in the United States</u>. 1991, Washington, D.C.: U.S. Department of Justice

Hayes, L. M. (1994). <u>Jail suicides: overcoming obstacles to prevention</u>: Crisis: The Journal of Crisis Intervention and Suicide Prevention, 15 (2)

Hayes, L. M. & Rowan, J.R. (1988). <u>National study of jail suicides: seven years later</u>. Alexandria, Virginia: National Center on Institutions and Alternatives. Sponsored by National Institute of Corrections, U.S. Department of Justice

National Commission on Correctional Health Care (1992). <u>Standards for health services in prisons</u>. (2nd ed.). Chicago, IL.

National Law Enforcement Technology Center, Rockville, MD, U.S. Department of Justice, Office of Justice Programs, National Institute of Justice, 1995

Office of the Correctional Investigator (2011-2014). <u>A three-year review of federal inmate suicides</u>. Office of the Correctional Investigator of Canada, Final Report September 10, 2014

Parkes, J.G. & Carson, R. (2008). <u>Sudden death during restraint: do some positions affect lung functions</u>? Medicine, Science and the Law 48 (2) 137-41

Parkes, J.G. Thake, D., & Price, M. (2011). <u>Effect of seated restraint and body size on lung function</u>. Medicine Science and the Law 51 (3) 177--81

Pearson, J. (August 26, 2014). AP Writer Peltz, J. and AP Researcher Shafner contributors. New York City Jail Investigations. Associated Press

Reay, D.T. (1996). Suspect restraint and sudden death. Law Enforcement Bulletin, Quantico, Va. FBI (http://wwwfbi.gov/publications//eb/1996/May 966.tx) - Retrieved 2014-12-18

Rowan, J. R. & Hayes, L. M. (1995). Training curriculum on suicide detection and prevention in jails and lockups. Mansfield, Mass: National Center on Institutions and Alternatives. Sponsored by National Institute of Corrections, U.S. Department of Justice

Seiter, R. P. (2011). Corrections and introduction (3rd ed.). New Jersey: Upper Saddle River, Pearson Education, Inc.

Stratton, S. J. Rogers, C. B. & Gruzaski, G. (2001). Factors associated with sudden death of individuals is requiring restraint for excited delirium. AM J Emergency Med 19 (3) 187-81

Chapter 10

INVESTIGATION OF INMATE-ON-INMATE SEXUAL ASSAULT

Chapter Learning Objectives

- Discuss the Prison Rape Elimination Act (PREA) of 2003, and requirements for prisons
- Define sexual abuse according to the PREA, 2003, Code of Federal Regulations (CFR) 115.6
- State how the PREA defines "prisons"
- Discuss the value of an objective classification system to identify predators and potential victims
- List staff and agency reporting duties according to CFR 115.61
- Explain the responsibilities of the investigating officer according to CFR 115.71
- Discuss the administrative investigation of inmate-on-inmate sexual assault according to CFR 115.71(f)
- Explain the required reporting procedures to inmates in accordance with CFR 115.73

Prior to beginning our discussion of inmate-on-inmate sexual assault I must remind the internal investigator that once the shift supervisor, administrator or investigator is notified of such incident, immediate notification should be made up the chain of command and to law enforcement officials. Law enforcement personnel specially trained in sexual assault cases should respond to the facility as soon as possible to commence the criminal investigation on the inmate allegation. Pursuant to the Prison Rape Elimination Act (2003b), National Standards, Code of Federal Regulations (CFR) 115.71(1), when an outside agency (or law enforcement officials) investigates allegations of sexual abuse, the facility should cooperate with outside investigators and should endeavor to remain informed about the progress of the investigation. The facility investigator will be assigned to accomplish the administrative investigation (CFR 115.71(f).

PREA of 2003, Public Law 108-79

The PREA (2003b), was passed in both houses of the U.S. Congress and signed by then President George W. Bush on September 4, 2003. The objective of the act is to curb prison sexual assault through "zero tolerance" policies. The Act also has national standards to prevent incidents of sexual violence in prisons. The law mandated the U.S. Department of Justice to make the prevention of sexual assault in prison a top priority in each prison system (Jordan, Morgan & McCampbell, 2006).

The PREA (2003a), provides national standards in the form of Code of Federal Regulations to provide guidelines to facilities for the prevention, detection, investigation and tracking of inmate sexual assaults. Some important goals of the PREA standards as reported by the Center for Innovative Public Policies (Retrieved 2014) are listed below:

- Address the detection, elimination and prevention of sexual assault and rape in correctional systems, including lock-ups operated by law enforcement agencies
- Direct collection and dissemination of information on the incidence of prisoner-on-prisoner sexual violence.
- Provide ways for agencies to improve their policies, procedures, directives, and operations to prevent and reduce the incidents of sexual abuse in their facilities.

Sexual Abuse CFR 115.6

According to CFR 115.6, sexual abuse of an inmate, detainee or resident by another inmate, detainee or resident includes any one of the following acts. If the victim does not consent, is compelled by force or threats into such act by overt or implied threats of violence, or is unable to consent or refuse.

1. Contact between the penis and the exterior genital organs of the female, including the labia majora, labia minora, clitoris and vestibule of the vagina, or the penis and the anus, including penetration, however, slight.
2. Contact between the mouth and the penis, anus or labia majora, labia minora, clitoris and/or vestibule of the vagina.
3. Entrance into the anal or genital opening of another person, however slight, by a hand, finger, object or other instrument.
4. Any other intentional touching, either directly or through the clothing, of the sex organs, anus, groin, breast, inner thigh or the buttocks of another person, excluding contact incidental to a physical altercation.

PREA Definition of Prisons

The PREA covers all adult male and female institutions as well as juvenile detention facilities. The PREA defines "prisons" in a broad sense to wit, *"any federal, state, or local confinement facility, including local detention facilities, police lock-ups, juvenile facilities and state and federal prisons".* The term "inmate" applies to any person held in a custodial setting for any duration by a prison as prison is defined by the PREA.

The Value of an Objective Classification System

Allen, Latessa & Ponder (2010), defines classification or risk assessment as the process of dividing an inmate population into manageable groups for custody and treatment purposes with the major goal to bring together persons roughly similar on such characteristics as aggressiveness, institutional history of a predatory nature against other inmates, perceived need for protection from other inmates, escape potential, need for treatment, gang affiliation and so on. The similar groups can then be assigned to custody level and treatment programs. Case in Point: As a new correctional officer in the early 1970s, I observed in one institution inmates with a predatory institutional history, perceived bullies, extortionist and highly assaultive inmates classified to administrative segregation after a reclassification hearing. What was amazing to see was that all of these so-called tough guys walked around each one afraid of the other person's reputation for violence; therefore, there was no apparent extortion, no bullying, and no assaults in administrative segregation all the inmates got along with few if any incidents. From this short case one can see the value of an objective and effective classification system.

For our purpose of preventing sexual abuse, an effective classification system will assign inmates to various housing pods or dormitories, and programming based on inmates' perceived level of risk and staff supervision necessary. Over a period time and based on inmate's record or newly discovered information, the inmate may be reclassified after a due process hearing to a higher or lower classification. An objective of classification is to assign dangerous or aggressive inmates to a high security classification thus increasing the safety, security and good order of the institution and attempting to keep predatory inmates from weaker victims. According to Stinchcomb and Fox (1999), classification serves to segregate the following:

- Pretrial detainees from convicted inmates
- Sentenced inmates from un-sentenced inmates
- Males from females
- Adults from juveniles
- Violent from non-violent inmates
- General population from special needs inmates (emotionally disturbed, elderly, physically disabled and so on)

Stinchomb and Fox (1999), reminds us that the classification process does not always work as intended, particularly when the detention center/prison is faced with severe overcrowding which may cause inmates to be placed wherever there is available space rather than where they can function best. In March v. Butler (2001), the court held that classification and risk assessment process does not adequately identify potential predators and potential victims. I submit that the process may not be perfect but it is the best process we have for now. In support of my submission Jones v. Clarke (1996), found that a lack of classification and risk assessment system constitutes deliberate indifference where inmates were harmed by other inmates because housing assignments did not account for the risk violent inmates posed.

Staff and Agency Reporting Duties

According to 28, CFR 115.61 (a), the agency shall require all staff to immediately report any knowledge, suspicions, or information regarding an incident of sexual abuse that occurred in a facility, whether or not it is part of the agency, retaliation against inmates or staff who reported the incident, any staff neglect or violation of responsibilities that may have contributed to an incident or retaliation. Additionally CFR 115.61 (b) requires that apart from reporting to designated supervisors or officials, staff shall not reveal any information related to a sexual abuse incident/report to anyone other than to the extent necessary, as should be specified in agency policy, to make treatment, investigation and other security and management decisions.

Unless otherwise precluded by federal, state or local law, medical and mental health practitioners shall be required to report sexual abuse as stipulated in the above paragraph, CFR 115.61 (a). And to inform inmates of the practitioner's duty to report, and the limitations of confidentiality (CFR 115.61 (c). If the alleged victim is under the age of 18 or considered a vulnerable adult under a state or local vulnerable persons statue (e.g. statutes against abuse of the elderly). The agency shall report the allegation to the designated state or local services agency under applicable state mandatory reporting laws. All allegations of sexual abuse including third party and anonymous reports shall be reported to the facility's designated investigators.

Pursuant to CFR 115.82, provisions shall be made for testing the inmate victim for sexual transmitted diseases (STDs), in addition, CFR 115.21 requires counseling for the treatment of STDs, if appropriate shall be provided. CFR 115.43 mandates that inmates at high risk for sexual victimization shall not be placed in involuntary protective custody unless an assessment of available alternatives has been conducted and it has been determined that there is no reasonable available alternative means of separation. Inmates may be placed in involuntary protective custody for less than 24 hours while an assessment is being completed. Every 30 days a classification hearing shall be held to afford such inmate a review to determine whether there is continuing need for protective custody (CFR 115.43).

Responsibilities of the Internal Investigating Officer

The investigation of sexual abuse allegations will take a different format than previously discussed throughout this book with other types of facility administrative investigations. Investigations shall be conducted pursuant to Title 28, Part 115 of the Code of Federal Regulations. The responsibilities of the investigating officer are contained in CFR 115.71, Criminal and Administrative Agency Investigations. CFR 115.71 requires investigations into allegations of sexual abuse and sexual harassment to be promptly, thoroughly and objectively investigated for all allegations, including third party and anonymous reports. CFR 115.34 requires the investigator to have received special training in sexual abuse. I began this chapter by stating that the investigation should be turned over to law enforcement personnel, specifically the sex offense or sex crimes unit which may be known by other names in other states.

CFR 115.34 (a) and (b) requires investigators to gather and preserve direct and circumstantial evidence (refer to Chapter 4 for definitions of direct and circumstantial evidence) including any available physical and DNA evidence and any available electronic monitoring data. The investigator shall interview alleged victim(s) suspected perpetrators and all witnesses. Prior complaints and reports of sexual abuse involving the suspected perpetrator(s) shall also be reviewed (CFR 115.71 c).

Relating to law enforcement investigators, when the quality of the evidence appears to a fair and reasonable person to support criminal prosecution, the agency shall conduct compelled interviews only after consulting with prosecutors as to whether compelled interviews may be an obstacle for subsequent prosecution. If the facility investigator derives newly discovered facts and evidence that supports criminal prosecution not known to law enforcement officials, sex crimes investigators should be contacted with the newly discovered information at once.

The credibility of an alleged inmate victim, suspect, or witness shall be assessed on an individual basis and shall not be determined by the person's status as inmate or staff. Remember in the eyes of the courts, an inmate's testimony is just as credible as an officer's testimony so long as there is some evidence to support either version. According to CFR 115.71 (e), the agency shall not require an inmate who alleges sexual abuse to submit to a polygraph examination or other truth-telling devices as a condition for proceeding with the investigation of the allegation.

Administrative Investigation

When possible an investigator of the same sex as the alleged victim should be the investigating officer;

Investigators shall conduct sexual abuse investigations promptly without regard for an inmate's sexual orientation, sex or gender identity;

Prior to transporting the alleged inmate victim to an outside hospital emergency room for evaluation and preparation of a rape kit or other examination, the inmate shall be instructed to remove one item of clothing at a time in order to collect any potential DNA evidence. Each item of clothing worn by the inmate should be placed in a paper bag along with the chain of evidence (chain of custody) form and container. Of course this evidence shall be turned over to the law enforcement sex offense unit;

If the inmate victim names the perpetrator or perpetrators the alleged inmate suspect's clothing also shall be removed and preserved as stated above for the inmate victim. Additionally, I recommend searching the suspect's cell for clothing (especially underwear that could very well contain DNA evidence) or other items that could possibly contain DNA evidence. All evidence should be turned over to law enforcement personnel for testing at their crime lab;

The crime scene shall be secured and access to the crime scene should be limited to law enforcement personnel, the facility investigator, and medical staff as needed. A log book shall be established and maintained by an officer of anyone entering and leaving the crime scene with the date and time. Law enforcement personnel will usually notify the facility investigator when to release the crime scene;

If the sexual abuse is not reported or discovered within a recent time frame the facility investigator shall secure the alleged crime scene with an officer and a log book as stated above and the alleged victim and alleged perpetrator(s) shall be immediately separated while under investigation. Facility medical services or in the absence of the availability of facility medical personnel, transport the inmate victim to a local hospital emergency room upon advisement of law enforcement personnel which could depend upon the date of the alleged incident. Confiscation of clothing and cell search from the alleged victim and suspect(s) shall be conducted as previously stated;

If the facility administrator does not object, it may be useful with an uncooperative inmate victim that does not wish to be labeled a snitch to make available to the him/her a victim advocate from a rape crisis center to visit the facility and interview the victim and document efforts to obtain assistance from that agency. I respectfully recommend obtaining a written report if possible, from the rape crisis center personnel of the interview conducted with the victim and, if possible, obtain a written report from the victim witnessed by the rape crisis center personnel;

If the victim refuses to cooperate with the investigation, the investigator should follow-up with any persons identified as having knowledge of the alleged incident. If no such persons are identified and the victim has previously been cooperative, the investigator should determine whether the victim has been threatened or coerced and whether the investigation should go forward without the victim's cooperation;

Additionally, CFR 115.71 (f), requires the administrative investigator to determine whether staff actions or failures to act contributed to the sexual abuse;

Document in a written report that includes a description of the physical and testimonial evidence, the reasoning behind credibility assessments, and investigation facts and findings;

Substantiated allegations of conduct that appears to be an apparent violation of state law shall be referred for prosecution;

The departure of the alleged perpetrator or victim from the facility does not provide a basis for terminating the investigation;

The facility investigator shall not impose an evidentiary standard higher than a "preponderance of the evidence" in determining whether allegations of sexual abuse is substantiated. A preponderance of available evidence refers to proof which leads a fair and reasonable investigator to find the existence of the allegation or charge in question is more probable than not.

The investigation report should include at a minimum, a narrative of the allegation(s), a comprehensive listing of factual findings, summarization of the important details of interviews with the victim, alleged perpetrator(s), witnesses, medical personnel, law enforcement personnel and possible rape crisis personnel, factual conclusions supported by some evidence, to wit, physical evidence, documentary evidence (eyewitness statements), DNA evidence, housing unit video recordings, and so on.

Some suggested recommendations that may be used by the internal facility investigator based upon the facts and evidence uncovered in the specific sexual abuse incident could include any of the following:

- Annual employee training specific to the prevention, identification, reporting and handling of inmate sexual abuse that includes indicators of inmate misconduct of a sexual nature.
- Providing the facility investigator with annual updated specialized training in sexual abuse investigation including the PREA Code of Federal Regulations standards
- Possible revisions to the detention center/prison classification system and procedures to identify potentially aggressive or vulnerable inmates to sexual abuse.
- Create a mechanism for inmates to confidentially report sexual abuse either as a victim, witness, complainant or anonymous confidential informant.
- Reclassification hearings to determine if the victim requires placement in protective custody.
- Revise agency policy to conform to the PREA of 2003, and relevant corrections case law as a proactive measure to ensure that inmates' constitutional right to be free from bodily harm by other inmates is safeguarded.
- Add cameras to blind areas of inmate housing units to capture actions of inmates and increase safety and security.
- Increase staffing in order to more effectively monitor housing units.

- Conduct a physical plant vulnerability assessment as a proactive strategy to determine which areas could facilitate possible sexual violence.
- Refer incident and evidence for criminal prosecution.
- Disciplinary action for any staff who displayed a deliberate indifference to inmate safety by actions of failure to act by specifying actions or inactions and policy violations that contributed to the sexual abuse.

Investigators should not shy away from making recommendations to prevent the incident from happening again that may require financial expenditures such as staffing, adding security cameras and so on. The facility administrator may even follow your suggestion. Case in Point: I conducted a physical plant vulnerability assessment of a jail annex which was previously an automobile dealership. I wrote the sheriff a detailed report of various ways and means an inmate could escape. The sheriff called me in and explained that he was not in the position to spend the money necessary to upgrade the building because he was in the process of building a brand new state of the art detention center as part of a federal court ruling. Approximately 60 days later an escape occurred on the midnight shift as I had foretold in my written report. Upon learning of the escape the sheriff angrily called me at my office and commanded me to report to him at once. Upon arriving at his office, he angrily demanded to know, "how could this have happened"? I pulled from my briefcase the physical plant vulnerability assessment and laid it in front of the sheriff. He quickly calmed down and said, "you did tell me that was going to happen if I didn't spend money on that old jail didn't you"? Then he made available most of the expenditures to upgrade the physical security of the detention center and said, "if the press knew you advised me beforehand and I didn't do anything, they would roast me". The crux of what I am saying is, call it like it is.

Required Reporting Procedures

Code of Federal Regulations 119.73 (a) requires that a report be made to inmates following an investigation into an inmate's allegation of sexual abuse. The regulation mandates that the agency inform the inmate as to whether the allegation has been determined to be substantiated, unsubstantiated, or unfounded. Failure to make the required notification could cause the facility administrator to be unnecessarily the recipient of inmate litigation for an 8th or 14th Amendment violation only to answer in volumes of unnecessary paperwork that the incident was in fact investigated and whatever the factual findings were.

Case in Point: Several female officers reported sexual harassment by male supervisors in a prison. The incident was investigated, determined to be founded and staff violators were appropriately disciplined; however, no one told the female complainants. Therefore, they commenced litigation and notified the local office of the Equal Employment Opportunity Commission (EEOC) thinking that the agency failed to take action amounting to condoning sexual harassment in violation of federal law. At the EEOC hearing prior to litigation, the females were shocked to learn that the incident was in fact investigated and disciplinary action up to an including termination was also accomplished but it was all held confidential. The female complainants said, "If you had only told us that you investigated it and disciplined the supervisors we would not have initiated any of these proceedings".

If the correctional agency chose not to conduct an internal investigation into the inmate's allegation, the correctional agency shall request information regarding the case reported to local law enforcement sexual offense investigators as to why the investigation was not conducted or closed and the factual reasons for doing so in order to inform the inmate (CFR 115.73 (b).

The inmate victim shall also be notified whenever the agency learns that the alleged abuser has been indicted by the grand jury or formally charged with the criminal offense within the facility (CFR 115.73 (d) (1). Or, the agency learns that the alleged perpetrator(s) has been convicted on the charge (CFR 115.73 (d) (1) (2). All such notifications and/or attempted notifications shall be documented (CFR 115.73 (e). The agency's obligation to report to the inmate under the standard CFR 115.73 shall terminate if the inmate is released from the agency's custody (CFR 115.73 (f).

References

Allen, H. E., Latessa, E. J. & Ponder, B. S. (2010). Corrections in America an introduction, (12ᵗʰ ed.). Upper Saddle River, N.J.: Pearson Prentice Hall

Jones v. Clarke, 94 F. 3d. 1191 (8ᵗʰ Cir. 1996).

Jordan, A. Morgan, M. & McCampbell, M. (2006). The Prison Rape Elimination Act : What Police Chiefs Need to Know. tp://policechiefmagazine.org/magazine.org/magazine/ index.cfm? The Police Chief, Volume 73, No. 4, April 2006, accessed November 22, 2014.

March v. Butler Cnty., ACA 268 F. 3d 1014 (11ᵗʰ Cir. 2001).

Prison Rape Elimination Act (2003a), (Public Law 108-79), United States Department of Justice, Wikipedia, the free encyclopedia (pdf). Retrieved 2014-11-24.

Prison Rape Elimination Act (2003b), Electronic Code of Federal Regulations, Title 28, Judicial Administration, Chapter 1, Part 115 - Prison Rape Elimination Act National Standards, U.S. Government Printing Office.

Stinchcomb, J. B. & Fox, V. B. (1999). Introduction to corrections, (5ᵗʰ ed.). New Jersey: Prentice Hall, Inc.

The Center for Innovative Public Policies. Police and law enforcement short-term holding facilities (lock-ups) & the Prison Rape Elimination Act. Information and Assistance for Law Enforcement & Chiefs of Police. (http://www.cipp.org/ sexual/index2.html) Retrieved 2014-11-22.

Chapter 11

INVESTIGATION OF INMATE INFRACTIONS

(Rule Violation Reports)

Chapter Learning Objectives

- Differentiate between minor and major infractions pursuant to ACA Standards
- State the duties of the investigating officer
- State the standard of proof used by the disciplinary officer or board
- Explain how the 5th Amendment to the U.S. Constitution affects disciplinary hearings

---

To begin with the investigator should not investigate any inmate infractions if the investigator is a participant or a witness. One's objectivity and partiality will be questioned and it is unethical to do so. Before beginning the investigation read the officer's report of infraction/rule violation and ensure that it is free from mistakes, errors, concise and reporting the facts as to: who, what, when, where, how, why and what actions taken and free from personal bias. If it is not correctly written return it to the officer at once for correction. In some jurisdictions, if the officer's report is not correctly completed including the correct rule violation, the disciplinary hearing officer or board will automatically throw

142

out the infraction. Ensure that the report contains only factual information.

Minor and Major Infractions

Some correctional agencies define infractions by major and minor, some by Grades I, II, III and so on. Additionally, all accredited correctional institutions operate according to the standards of the American Correctional Association; therefore, this book will use the ACA terminology of "Major infractions" and "Minor Infractions". A major infraction is any facility rule violation that has serious inmate and facility management implications. Major rule violations should be handled through the formal disciplinary process and/ or referral for possible prosecution, or both depending upon the seriousness of the incident and possible violation of state law. An inmate may be placed in disciplinary detention for a major rule violation after being found guilty at a hearing. The correctional agency's policy and inmate rule book should determine the specific actions that constitute all major rule violations.

Minor infractions which do not have serious inmate and/or facility management implications, may be resolved through an informal facility process that includes providing the inmate with a written statement of the violation and a decision by the hearing board within seven days. Inmates are not usually transferred to disciplinary detention for minor rule violations. Facility policy should determine the specific actions that constitute all minor violations of facility policy.

Duties of Investigating Officer

Pursuant to the landmark case on inmate disciplinary proceedings, to wit, Wolff v. McDonnell (1974), inmates have procedural due process rights, that is, the inmate shall receive advanced written notice of the specific rule violation filed against him/her and any details of the charges against him/her;

The above notice will be given to the inmate within 24 hours of the time that the rule violation report is filed, unless the charge is dismissed informally. In addition, the investigating officer should ensure that the inmate has received information regarding any evidence supporting the charge;

The investigator should notify the inmate that he/she has a right to present evidence and call witnesses on his behalf (Tolden v. Coughlin, 1982) so long as it is not unduly hazardous to institutional safety, security and good order;

In order for the inmate to prepare his defense the investigator should remind the inmate (as should be stipulated in the inmate handbook) that they may avail themselves to counsel (not attorneys), namely, jail house lawyers, or use of counsel substitute (usually a correctional officer but can be another inmate if requested) to provide assistance for some inmates who may be semi-illiterate or otherwise cannot understand the proceedings (Lee v. Coughlin, 1998; Ayers v. Ryan, 1998).

The supervisor required to conduct the investigation will interview inmate charged with the rule violation and any other inmate(s) who may be participants or witnesses as soon as possible and record the inmates' testimony for further review and evaluation. In addition to oral testimony from witnesses, written statements should also be taken and when appropriate, supplemental reports prepared to resolve any inconsistencies. If the investigator receives information from a confidential informant, the inmate charged with a rule violation does not have a right to read the confidential informant's report. In re: Dawson v. Smith (1983), the U. S. Appeals Court found no violation of an inmate's due process rights when he was denied access to a report by a confidential informant because access would risk retaliation against the informant especially since the report proved to be reliable and was supported by evidence. Investigators are well aware that obtaining reliable information is difficult enough without putting the investigator's reliable confidential inmate information network at risk. The key for the investigator is that he cannot just state that the information is reliable, there must be evidence to show that the information is reliable in order to be used at a disciplinary hearing (Shumway v. Oregon State Penitentiary (1983).

The investigation shall be completed within 72 hours excluding weekends and holidays; if the facts and circumstances at issue warrant, the investigator may choose to continue the investigation to obtain additional information, referring the matter for possible prosecution, referring the matter for a full disciplinary committee hearing, or informally resolving the charge. The informal process includes providing the inmate with a written statement of the rule violated and a decision by the investigating officer within seven business days as would be the case of resolving a minor rule violation. If an incident is informally resolved, a memorandum shall be placed in the inmate's central file briefly describing the incident and the reason for informal adjudication (ACA Guidelines, 1991);

After interviewing the inmate, staff, inmate witnesses, examining and securing all physical evidence or contraband (including photographs), the investigator will determine if there is reasonable cause to proceed with the disciplinary proceedings;

Based upon an evaluation of all the evidence, facts and circumstances, if the investigator should determine that no disciplinary action is warranted and no hearing is recommended there should be a place on the form to so indicate, if not, the investigator should state that as part of his or her investigation along with the evidentiary reasons why.

Investigators should not create a lot of unnecessary work for themselves when the officer has physical evidence to support the disciplinary report. Regarding officers witnessing inmate misbehavior reports in People Ex Rel Vega v. Smith (1985), the high court of New York found that misbehavior reports signed by correctional staff were sufficient to reach a determination of guilt without the officer's presence. Due process mandates are satisfied when staff reports specify an incident that is a violation of written inmate rules of discipline, the reports are dated on the same day as the violation occurred, the report(s) is endorsed or initialed by one or more other correctional staff, the inmate is offered assistance in preparing for the hearing, no witnesses are requested in advance, and the inmate offers little more than a denial of the charge;

The Maryland Office of the Secretary of State summarizes the tasks and responsibilities of the investigating officer as they see it as follows:

Date and time of violation;

Location of the alleged violation;

Identification of inmate accused of committing the rule violation;

Identify witnesses;

Determine the facts, circumstances, and mitigating factors of the alleged rule violation;

Determine the appropriate rule violation that should be charged;

Preserve physical evidence;

Make recommendation to dismiss, handle informally or send to disciplinary hearing officer or board.

Standard of Proof

In Superintendent v. Hill (1985), the court stated the standard of proof to be used in disciplinary hearings, namely, *"some evidence"* must be shown for each disciplinary violation charged. Additionally, the disciplinary hearing officer or board's decision must be based on the evidence in the record. This some evidence rule has been challenged across the U.S. The Vermont Supreme Court ruled in LeFaso v. Patiss(1993), that the "some evidence" standard violates due process and that a "preponderance of the evidence" standard is required at prison disciplinary hearings. Referring to <u>Superintendent, Massachusetts Correctional Institution v. Hill</u> (1985), summarizing the U.S. Supreme Court as the court posed the question: Why do states continue to go back and forth on this same issue of standard of proof in inmate disciplinary hearings when we have already decided the case in <u>Superintendent, Massachusetts Correctional Institution v. Hill</u> (1985) that prison authorities need only have "some evidence" that an inmate committed a disciplinary infraction to satisfy due process", (Stare Decisis - stand by that which has already been decided)? Some states even use the standard: "sufficient evidence" to make the hearing officer believe that the inmate committed the alleged violation. All of the above have one thing in common and that is, the investigator should forward evidence, to wit, eyewitness statements, physical evidence, documentary evidence and so on that the alleged violation did in fact occur as reported by the officer.

The Fifth Amendment and Disciplinary Hearings

Inmates charged with a rule violation have a constitutional right under the 5th Amendment to the U.S. Constitution to remain silent. According to <u>Baxter v. Palmgiano</u>, (1976), an adverse inference can be drawn from an inmate's silence during the investigation and during the disciplinary proceeding. Investigators should be aware that the inmate's silence alone may not be used to support a conclusion or a disciplinary hearing officer's finding that the inmate did in fact commit the prohibited act to which he was charged (Lewisburg Prison Project, 2002).

References:

American Correctional Association (August, 1991). <u>Guidelines for the development of policies & procedures</u>, Adult Correctional Institutions. Laurel, MD, 245-253.

Ayers v. Ryan, 152 F. 2nd 77 (2nd Cir. 1988).

Baxter v. Palmgiano, 425 (U.S. 308, L., 1976).

Dawson v. Smith, 719 F. 2d 896 (7th Cir. 1983).

Lee v. Coughlin, 26 F. Supp 2d 615 (S. D. N. Y. 1998).

Lefaso v. Patise, 91-581, 161 Vt. 46, 630 A. 2d 695 (1993).

Lewisburg Prison Project, Inc. Legal Bulletin 6.1, Disciplinary hearings (May 2002), Lewisburg, PA.

Maryland Office of the Secretary of State, Division of State Documents, Investigating and reporting an inmate rule violation (12.02.27.05. (undated) Annapolis, MD.

People Ex Rel Vega v. Smith, 485 N.E. 2d 997 (N.Y. 1985).

Shumway v. Oregon State Penitentiary, 657 F. 2d 686 (Ore. 1983).

Superintendent v. Hill, 472, U.S. 444 (1985).

Superintendent, Massachusetts Correctional Institution v. Hill, 472 U.S. 445 (1985).

Tolden v. Coughlin 457 N.Y.S. 2d 942 (App. Div. N.Y. 1982).

Wolff v. McDonnell, 418 U.S. 539 (1974).

Chapter 12

INVESTIGATION OF COMMON INMATE INJURY REPORTS

Chapter Learning Objectives

- List some common inmate injuries
- State and discuss the elements of a personal injury claim
- Briefly discuss U. S. Supreme Court and State Court decisions on inmate injuries
- State what the investigator should look for in the details of the inmate injury report
- Identify and discuss the investigation procedures to be followed when investigating common inmate injury reports

---

The detention center and/or prison has an obligation of reasonable care to protect inmates from unnecessary injuries. Some inmate injuries are legitimate and some are not. One will always find some inmates who wish to be unjustly enriched at the expense of the correctional institution, county and/or city. Especially if there is an unsafe condition on an officer's post that has not been reported or addressed by the staff and an inmate knowingly injures himself so that he can be duly compensated. At other times, some inmates may injure themselves in order to seek litigation and financial compensation especially if the agency has made financial settlements in the past with other inmates out of court. Some injuries may be legitimate such as injuries that occurred while working in the kitchen, facility maintenance, operating various types of machinery and so on.

There are many injuries which may appear suspicious on their face. As stated by a federal judge most people do not just fall out of bed or fall face first into walls or lockers. The natural inclination is to put out one's hands to break a fall. Also, most inmates do not just walk into a door or wall and receive the injuries they sustain. In many of these cases, the injury may be the result of an inmate fight, a gang assault on an inmate victim, self-mutilation or an unreported use of force by staff. It is the investigator's task to find out how the inmate sustained any such injury.

Common Inmate Injuries

Some common inmate injuries that may occur as stated by Calisi (2014), and that may subject the correctional facility to litigation, involving inmate work assignments are: Food service areas, laundry, maintenance of the physical plant, motor vehicle maintenance, construction, correction industries and so on. Injuries can range from cuts and bruises to serious burns, broken or fractured bones, injuries to the head and more. One of the inmate's favorite causes for litigation is when being transported by officers, they are involved in a motor vehicle accident. Personal injury attorneys may remind facility administrators that when inmates are passengers in a motor vehicle (automobile, van, bus, etc.) accident the inmate has a right to pursue an injury claim against the correctional institution. Of course local law enforcement will prepare accident reports and may issue any traffic citations to the transporting officer or another involved vehicle operator. If you are asked to investigate a motor vehicle accident for policy and procedure compliance and safety and security during transport, if possible, obtain a copy of the police accident report, it will be most useful during your investigation. If law enforcement personnel determine that the transport officer was at fault or negligent, your investigation must certainly include that information along with recommendations for possible disciplinary action.

One of the most common forms of pretrial detainee and prison inmate injuries is inmate-on-inmate assault and battery. These assaults include injuries sustained from sharp weapons and blunt instrument trauma. Although detention center/prison officials may not be at fault for inmate-on-inmate assaults, officials can become liable for failure to protect, lack of officer supervision, failure to properly classify predatory assaultive inmates and failure to anticipate an assault. Federal inmates file injury claims by following the procedures in the Federal Tort Claims Act. Pretrial detainees and state sentenced inmates file their injury claims by following the procedures listed in individual states' Tort Claims Act (Calisi, 2014).

Elements of a Personal Injury Claim

Calisi (2014), states that for the inmate to succeed in a personal injury federal or state tort claim the inmate must prove three elements as listed below. Additionally, unless the inmate can prove all three elements his claim of injury will be unsuccessful. The inmate has an obligation to show that the facility's negligence caused the verifiable injury:

1. The facility breached its obligation or duty to care;
2. How the negligent act (breach) occurred;
3. The negligence resulted in verifiable injuries or damages.

For the inmate (or his attorney) to prove the above three elements requires evidence. Your report of investigation of the alleged injury may prove crucial to their case and the correctional agency's defense. In Chapter 4, the significance of documenting physical evidence by photographing was discussed. Use the facility's camera to document the alleged cause of the injury and the actual injury itself. A word of caution, when I photograph inmate injuries, I photograph the actual injury at the facility medical clinic or hospital not blood that is everywhere so that one cannot see the actual injury. It can be misleading to the reviewer of your report to see a lot of blood but not the size of the actual injury causing the bleeding. As you are aware sometimes one can get a small cut that bleeds profusely especially if one is on blood thinners. After medical professionals clean away the blood the investigator may be looking at a very small cut that does not pose a serious physical injury.

Since most contemporary correctional institutions have the capacity to videotape various areas of the facility on a twenty-four hour basis, this should be one of the first pieces of evidence that the investigator should review in anticipation that the video system has captured the alleged incident. In case the video has in fact captured the incident safeguard the video in the Chief of Security's safe or the Deputy Warden of Security's safe for possible future litigation. Have a copy of the video reproduced on a compact disc and forward the copy as an attachment to your report of investigation. Your report of investigation must discuss your review of the videotape with specific detail of what the video documented.

The investigator should carefully analyze inmate eyewitness reports supporting the inmate's claim. As previously stated, was the inmate witness in a position to observe what he has reported in favor of the claimant or is he relying on hearsay? Did any inmates or staff previously report a dangerous condition or danger in operating a particular machine? If an officer knew of a dangerous condition of should have known and took no action to eliminate it, to wit, have an inmate mop a wet floor and post a wet floor sign etc. or post a warning sign and not permit inmates to operate dangerous machines or otherwise allowed a dangerous condition to exist on his or her post or work area. Your investigation which is an objective quest for truth must so state this information and evidence along with a possible recommendation for disciplinary action of the officer for allowing a dangerous condition to exist on his or her post or work assignment area.

U. S. Supreme Court &
State Court Decisions on Inmate Injuries

In <u>Farmer v. Brennan</u> (1994), the U.S. Supreme Court held that only the unnecessary and wanton affliction of pain implicates and 8th Amendment violation. The court also classified its "deliberate indifference" standard after various courts of appeals adopted inconsistent tests while interpreting the standard. The court adopted a subjective test holding that prison officials cannot be found liable under the 8th Amendment for denying an inmate humane conditions of confinement unless the official knows of and completely disregards an excessive risk to inmate health or safety. Prison officials must be both aware of facts from which the inference could be drawn that is a substantial risk of a serious harm exists, and he must also draw the inference (Dougherty, 2008). "For a claim to be presented the inmate must show that he was incarcerated under conditions posing a substantial risk of serious harm, this is the objective test" (Allen, Latessa & Ponder, 2010, p. 297). According to Allen, Latessa & Ponder, (2010), under the former deliberate indifference test: Did prison officials act with a sufficiently culpable mental state? For a claim based on failure to prevent harm the complainant must show that he or she was incarcerated under conditions posing a substantial risk of serious harm. Under the objective test the culpable mental state (state of mind) requirement follows from the several Supreme Court decisions that only the unnecessary and wanton infliction of pain implicates the 8th Amendment.

In <u>Arnold v. South Carolina Department of Correction</u>, 1994, the U.S. Supreme Court did not consider whether inmate injuries caused by the operation of malfunctioning prison equipment fell within the domain of the 8th Amendment. Dougherty (2008), reporting on the Arnold case states that lower courts have differing opinions regarding whether or not malfunctioning prison and work place safety cases rise to the level of an 8th Amendment violation. The decisions range from finding no constitutional violation even when prison officials are aware of unsafe conditions to some courts also holding that prison official's knowledge of hazardous workplace conditions did not constitute deliberate indifference.

What Investigator Should Look for in the Inmate Injury Report

The inmate injury report either computerized or in hard copy form should state the essential: who, what, when, where, how, why, and what action taken by the officer but not necessarily in that order.

WHO?

Was the inmate allegedly injured, identify the inmate along with his/her identification number. Identify all staff and inmate witnesses to the alleged injury.

WHAT?

Specifically what happened. Example: inmate reports that he slipped and fell in the kitchen in front of the dishwasher. Or, inmate reports that he cut his right thumb on the meat slicer because he forgot to engage the hand safety mechanism and so on.

WHEN?

Date and time of the inmate's alleged injury, the date and time he/she reported it to an officer or supervisor. Date and time medical personnel were notified and inmate escorted to facility medical personnel for treatment or outside hospital.

WHERE?

Specific location of alleged injury and/or specific location of machinery along with machine serial number.

HOW?

Narrative of the incident as to how the incident occurred supported by inmate and staff eyewitness statements if possible. Also, supported by possible photographs, video recordings, sketches medical reports diagnosis and treatment and maintenance reports.

WHY?

State the conditions or contributing factors that caused the injury.

WHAT ACTIONS TAKEN?

The stated actions taken by the officer when he or she became aware of the alleged inmate injury. For example, the assigned kitchen security officer, John Doe, Shield Number 0000, reports that he immediately grabbed a clean towel out of the laundry cart and told the inmate to apply direct pressure to the wound to stop the bleeding, while the officer notified facility medical personnel.

Most jurisdictions will have the inmate sign that he did in fact receive medical treatment for the alleged injury or he refused treatment. The inmate cannot be the ultimate judge of what medical treatment is necessary or proper that is left to state licensed medical personnel.

Investigation Procedures

As soon as possible quickly visit the scene of the alleged incident and look for any physical evidence, namely, wet floor, damaged or malfunctioning equipment (photograph the scene) and any other physical evidence.

State who the investigator interviewed, what they verbally reported and obtain a written report from inmate victim, alleged eyewitnesses and staff eyewitnesses and the staff member on whose assigned post the incident occurred.

As previously stated, and if available, review the facility 24-hour video recording of the area and state what the video shows that is, consistency with the inmate's report or inconsistency.

Address and resolve if possible any and all inconsistencies between the injured inmate's report, inmate eyewitnesses' accounts and staff accounts of the incident.

State whether or not the staff or inmate victim was aware of the unsafe condition prior to the inmate's alleged injury.

State whether or not any staff members or inmates previously reported the alleged unsafe condition or machinery, date, time, name of individual reporting, if it was reported what preventive action was taken to eliminate the dangerous condition. If reported and a facility work order was prepared, obtain a statement from the maintenance unit as to what actions were taken to immediately repair the item or to make the unsafe condition inaccessible to anyone until maintenance had time to repair it.

State if the injury sustained by the inmate is consistent with medical prognosis and evaluation.

Examine the inmate training record and state whether or not the inmate received safety training for the machine that he was operating or safety training in other areas as a proactive measure to prevent injuries. State whether or not inmate followed safety training.

State the findings and conclusions derived from an evaluation of physical evidence, documentary evidence, video and photographic evidence, medical and any other evidence.

State the investigator's recommendations to prevent this type of incident from recurring again.

References

Allen, H. E. Latessa, E.J. & Ponder, B. S. (2010). <u>Corrections in America</u>, An Introduction (12th ed.) Upper Saddle River, N.J.: Pearson Prentice Hall

Arnold v. South Carolina Department of Corrections, 843, F. Supp. 110, 113 (D. S.C. 1994)

Calisi, Anthony P. (Judge), (2014). <u>Prison inmate injury claims & dangerous jail conditions</u>. (<u>http://www.injuryclaimcoach.com/ prison-inmate-injury.html</u>. - Retrieved Nov. 22, 2014.

Dougherty, C. (2008). <u>The cruel and unusual irony of prisoner work related injuries in the U. S.</u> University of Pennsylvania Law School, J.D. Candidate (scholar.law.upenn.edu/Cgi/vie wcontent,cg?articles=1305&context100-Similar) – Retrieved 2014-12-05

Farmer v. Brennan, 511, U.S. 825, 832 (1994)